Straight Talk:

Families Speak to Families about Child and Youth Mental Health

Conni Wells

Straight Talk: Families Speak to Families about Child and Youth Mental Health is a comprehensive step-by-step guide for families of children and youth with emotional, behavioral, and mental health disorders. This book is designed to assist families to navigate the many facets of the system of care and to build a balance between meeting the needs of their child or youth and those of parents and their family. Through the advice and the words of families, this guide addresses issues that have impacted families for decades but are often overlooked or not discussed by professionals. These issues include family emotions, telling others, dealing with stress, keeping a job, suicide, treatments, school, and more.

Citation: Wells, C., Straight Talk: Families Speak to Families about Child and Youth Mental Health. Axis Group Publishing, Axis Group I, LLC, Butler TN 2010

Acknowledgements

The Four Million...

Researchers estimate that there are over 4 million children and youth in the United States with an emotional, behavioral, or mental health disorder. That means there are over 4 million families who have experience, expertise, and support to offer the system and the families they serve based upon the realities of raising a child or youth with an emotional, behavioral, or mental health disorder.

For the past 30 years I have learned from the 4 million, admired their resilience, and cataloged their survival tactics; hoping to pass them forward to help other families and their children and youth. My gratitude and thanks to those families that have shown me how to navigate the mental health system; a lesson that is best taught by those that have first hand experience.

My deepest gratitude goes to John Reiss, friend, professional, and parent of a young adult with a mental health disorder; for his time and dedication in reviewing the final draft, making suggestions that made the text clearer and easier to understand, and cheering me on toward completion.

I also want to thank others that reviewed the book and contributed their ideas and suggestions; Jeremy Weaver, Therapeutic Day Counselor from Damascus, VA and James Taylor, MA. Ed., School Behavior Analyst in Statesboro, GA. Their personal and professional validation kept the project alive.

Finally, my thanks to Lindsay and Bug, whose lives are a daily reminder of the gap between a family doing their best and the system's ability to respond with the services and supports that are critical to survival.

This book is dedicated to the four million and their children and youth. It is their book...it is their words...I am only the medium.

Table of Contents

Introduction

He Smiles Anyway

When he was very young he cried so hard for so long that his vocal cords were damaged. **He smiles anyway...**

He was locked in a bathroom for hours at one day care center and kicked out of another when he was less than two years old. **He smiles anyway...**

The medication he takes makes his body twitch and jerk, even while he sleeps. **He smiles anyway...**

Some kids bully and make fun of him. Once they made him lick juice off the locker room floor. **He smiles anyway...**

Each day is a challenge to manage the memories, the meds, the people, the twitching, the demands, the behavior, and still get a night's sleep. **He smiles anyway...**

The smile lies...

This book was inspired by kids like AJ and their families. It was written through the voice of hundreds of families. It is intended to enlighten, teach, inspire, and sustain families as they deal with the emotional, behavioral, and mental health needs of their child or youth. This book is a connection between families who have never met one another but are linked through life circumstance; the emotional, behavioral, or mental health disorder of their child or youth.

Reading or Using This Book

We imagine that you will read this book starting where you need it the most. It may be in the front, middle, or you may be searching for information on a specific treatment, which is found near the back. Use it however meets your needs. The quotes are from families like you. The ideas, tips, forms and questions come from families as well.

This is…Straight Talk: Families Speak to Families about Child and Youth Mental Health.

***Straight Talk is a sharing of ideas with the understanding that not everything works for everyone. This should not be used as and is not a replacement for professional assistance. Anytime you feel that you or your child or youth are not doing as well as expected, please call one of the professionals on your team immediately. If you do not know who to call, seek assistance from a local support group or hospital or call 911 if it is an emergency.

Spotlight on Your Family

What is a family? I don't even know anymore. We have been pulled in a million different directions since Tara became sick. Our whole lives revolve around her, not us. My other kids are mad and hate her and what she does, my husband is about to leave us, and I really don't care about anything anymore. It's probably not normal to feel like this, but we aren't normal, so that doesn't count here."

Families face a multitude of frustrations but also experience many joys in raising their children and youth. Those frustrations may seem never ending and the joys much too far apart when you have a child or youth with mental, emotional, or behavioral issues. This section looks at how having a child with special emotional or mental health needs can impact your entire family.

New Beginnings

"We couldn't believe what we were hearing. I kept asking the same questions over and over. Not because I didn't understand but because I had no idea of what else to say."

Once you discover that your child or youth has an emotional or mental disorder, your life will change. This may happen slowly, or may hit like a lightning bolt. Many of you knew your child had problems long before you were told by a professional. Your life becomes full of therapy, special teachers, IEP's, doctors, medication, and even a new language! But, many families discover that they eventually adapt to their new life. Finally, your definition of a normal family changes, and you learn what is "normal for your family". But the best thing you can do for your child and family is to move into your new "normal" as soon as possible.

Some things in your family that might change as a result of your child's or youth's problems:

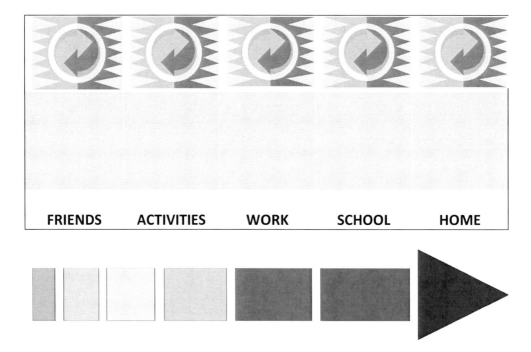

FRIENDS   ACTIVITIES   WORK   SCHOOL   HOME

 **TRY THIS...**

- **Educate yourself** and learn all you can about your child's or youth's condition.

- **Learn how to react** to your child's or youth's problems in as calm a manner as possible. This not only helps your child or youth, but also reduces the stress you experience each time you get upset.

- Start **looking for and taking joy in small improvements or accomplishments** in your child or youth.

- **Locate other parents** who have children with mental, emotional, or behavioral needs and support one another.

- **Keep doing the things in your life that you find enjoyable** such as sports, sewing, or visiting friends.

- Learn to **separate yourself from your child's or youth's disorder**, but not your child or youth.

- Remember that the emotional or mental disorder belongs to your child or youth. **You cannot make it go away** or take ownership of it.

- **Keep up family traditions**, vacations, and other celebrations to the extent possible. It is important to make sure that your family continues and life doesn't stop for everyone. Take mini-vacations, if necessary, but be sure that you haven't sacrificed the entire family's life on your child or youth.

- **Have weekly family meetings** to discuss what is happening and share ideas on what the family should do in the upcoming week. This is a time for everyone to participate and express their feelings and share accomplishments.

Balancing a Job and Your Child's Needs

"I loved my job. They were good about it for a long time. Then, leaving for appointments and meetings started to be a problem. I tried to explain, but I think they were just tired of the excuses."

Getting your family back into a routine may be challenging. In the middle of dealing with each crisis, being a parent or caretaker, and keeping the family together; you may also be trying to hold onto your job. Families often share that they have problems at work resulting from excessive absences due to picking up their child or youth from school when in trouble, going to meetings, and taking them to therapy or the doctor. Some employers are sensitive to problems, but others do not understand the demands or issues you have to deal with. It is important that you do everything you can to help them understand your needs and how this may impact your job, and to keep them updated on what is happening so they do not think your absences are simply because you do not want the job.

TRY THIS...

- Bring in a fact sheet and other information about your child's or youth's diagnosis to **help them understand** the problem and how it impacts your family.

- **Show them** that you can do a good job, but that you need their support in making the best of the situation.

- Schedule appointments and **meetings around work schedules** or when there is less demand in your workplace, such as during lunch, late in the day, or when work is generally slow.

- Give them brief information after each appointment to **keep them updated** and make them feel like a part of the solution.

- Meet with your boss regularly to **discuss how you can do well** at work despite the demands of your family.

You and Your Emotions

"It took us a year....but I finally feel like I have a grip on my feelings. For a while it felt like I needed to be in the hospital too. But I have learned that these emotional ups and downs just go with the job. I am not always in control, but most of the time I can at least talk about what I feel. A year ago that was impossible."

No one can be prepared for having a child or youth with an emotional, behavioral or mental health disorder. It can happen to any family, to any parent, in any social circle. It cuts across all cultures and economic levels. The self-confident parent, the model family, the teacher, preacher, and doctor can have a child or youth with emotional or mental health problems. Because it can hit anyone, anytime, anywhere, it is impossible to prepare for it. The best you can do is deal with your emotions one at a time and one day at a time.

Some feelings you may experience:

- **Shame or guilt:** You may feel that you somehow let your child or youth down and failed as a parent. This common feeling is hard to escape when others keep asking what you did wrong.
- **Sorrow:** You may be sad over the loss of the dreams you had for your child. You may remember days when your child or youth seemed happier, showed more emotion, or seemed to be more like other kids.
- **Anger:** You may be very angry when you have tried hard and feel you failed anyway. You may be angry at the way in which your child was diagnosed or the way you have to fight for services.
- **Depression:** You may feel depressed and overwhelmed by all that has happened. It is not unusual to feel that the burden is too great and to have a feeling of helplessness take over.
- **Fear**: You may fear for your child's or youth's life or future; you may fear for your own or other family member's lives; or you may have a fear of the future and what it holds.
- **Withdrawal**: It is common for families to withdraw not only from their community, but also from their child or youth. When you

have been hurt over and over again, it seems natural to start moving away from whatever is causing you pain.

Because mental illness symptoms may come and go unpredictably, you may find that you jump from one emotion to another, with little relief. People spend years trying to understand why this happened to their family. It is best to acknowledge your feelings and accept that there will be good days and bad days. Don't let your emotions run you; instead try to accept these feelings and take what you can from them. They are a part of your life.

 # TRY THIS...

- **Keep a journal** of your feelings. By pouring your heart out on paper you are letting go of some of the feelings that seem bottled up inside of you.

- **Keep a scrapbook** of the wonderful times your family has (only put in happy things) and read it on a regular basis or when you feel overwhelmed. This will remind you of the good times and help you look forward.

- Join an online social networking group such as Face Book. You can **interact with others**, share your experiences, and gain encouragement in a very private way.

- Join a chat group where you and other families of children and youth with mental, emotional, and behavioral needs can **share and support** one another online.

- Choose a good friend with whom you can **be honest about your feelings**. Tell them when you are sad, call when you feel depressed, and describe how you feel. It helps to acknowledge your feelings and talk about them out loud. Pick someone who is a great listener, is not judgmental, and does not tell you how to fix things.

- Decide that for every bad feeling you have, you are going to **search for a good one**. Sometimes when things are tough, it is hard to recognize good feelings and you will need to work in locating them.

- **Ask for professional help** in dealing with your feelings. Do not let your child's or youth's mental health issues make you emotionally ill. Ask one of the professionals who cares for your child or youth where <u>you</u> can get help.

- If you feel as though life is not worth living, GET HELP IMMEDIATELY. Feeling as though life is not worth living is an emergency. **Call for help** from a family member, friend, or professional.

Your Family Has Special Needs Too

"They told us she had a serious emotional disorder and that she would need to be in the hospital for a very long time. Then they asked if we knew what we needed. I didn't have a clue. I mean, I only had a kid with special needs for about a total of five minutes. They must have known how I felt because they gave us information and would ask us all the time what we needed. That was great, because each day it seemed we needed something new."

Finding out that your child or youth has an emotional or mental health disorder can have a profound effect on your entire family. There may have been confusing periods when no one believed that your child had a problem, or times when your family was blamed for your child's problems or the diagnosis took a long time to get. The time of diagnosis is a period when your family is vulnerable and probably feels very fragile. Your needs have changed, and you wonder if things will ever be the same again. Things may be so different, that you may wonder if you even know what your needs are.

Many families share that, after a time, their lives start to settle down. You will shift into a routine that feels "normal" for you. This is different for each family and there is no set deadline by which you should begin a new and predictable routine. Of course, with each day, it seems that something new pops up and you have to re-adjust.

WHAT SOME FAMILIES FEEL THEY NEED
Some families say that they would like:
- Someone to talk to who will listen without judging.
- Someone who is willing to let them cry, be angry, rant, or be in a bad mood for a while.
- Information about their child's or youth's problem presented in a way that they can understand.
- Recognition of all that they have done for their child.
- Honest information about what the future might hold for them and their child or youth.

- Someone to help them explain what is happening to the rest of their family.
- Someone who believes in them, their beliefs, and their ideas.
- Respect as a member of their child's or youth's care team.
- Access to information, evaluations, and assessments related to their child or youth.
- Someone they can count on to be "on their side", no matter what happens.
- Professionals who see them as a part of the solution, rather than a part of the problem.
- Professionals who look at the needs of the whole family, not just one child or youth.

If you feel that your family has some needs that are not being met, discuss them with a professional or friend. Let them know exactly what you think would help you and your family. Discuss this often so your needs become an accepted part of everyday life.

TRY THIS...

- **Write down what you feel is needed** and take a copy of this list to your next appointment. Turn it in at the beginning of the appointment to allow the staff time to review the list and gather information or resources for you.

- Set aside a regular time to talk with your family about what is happening and **brainstorm ideas** that each member feels might help.

- Make an appointment to **discuss what the family needs** in addition to what your child or youth needs. Check ahead of time to see if a discussion of family needs is something that is part of the program, or if you will be billed for it.

- Use the Checklist of Needs (This checklist is on the next page.) to **help professionals** working with your family to better understand how they can help you and your family.

 **Checklist of Needs**

Need	Urgency			Notes
	Needed NOW	Can Wait 1 Week	Just Wondering	Details on what is needed, who will help, notes about where to go or resources
For My Child/Youth				
Services (such as counseling, inpatient, outpatient, etc.)				
Payment for services (insurance, Medicaid, etc.)				
Information on disorder				
Education information (special education, IEP's, etc.)				
Recreation resources				
Treatment information				
Medication information				
Community programs				
Juvenile justice				
Others (list):				
For Our Family				
Housing				
Food				
Utilities (electricity, water, etc.)				
Transportation				
Employment				
Clothing				
Counseling				
Community programs				
Support (for other children, parent to parent, etc.)				
Help with paperwork				
Others (list):				

Your Other Children's Needs

"I want our family to be back to normal again. Like before Jim went to the hospital. Dad took us fishing, mom was happy, and I could go places with Jim. It's all gone now. My parents cry at night, especially since he was arrested. They seem different. I liked it when Jim was in jail; at least he wasn't here to cause a bunch of trouble. I could have my friends over and not worry about what he might say and do. I wonder when it will all stop."

When something disrupts one member of your family, it will likely upset the others. Brothers and sisters will each have feelings about what is happening in the family. Because so much time and concern is focused on the child or youth with problems, they may feel forgotten. Although they are not forgotten, there just is not enough time to go around.

Some of the feelings your other children may be experiencing include:

Anger	Your other children may be angry at the way their brother or sister acts or behaves. They may have had their belongings ruined or see how you are hurt by what is happening.
Embarrassment	Your child or youth with emotional, behavioral, or mental health issues may have acted out in public. Or, they may act badly at home or might "explode" in front of others. Your other children may not feel comfortable going out with them or having friends over to the house.
Jealousy	A child or youth with special needs may get a lot of time and attention. There are doctor's appointments, special programs, and everyone asks how they are doing. This attention may make your other children jealous.
Sadness	Your other children may be very sad at what has happened to the family. They may grieve, but not know how to handle or get over their sadness. They may be sad and not know why.

Guilt	Children might feel guilty for bad things that happen in the family. They may have thought something bad or wished that something bad would happen to another member. When it does, they may think it is their fault.
Fear	Your other children may be afraid of their brother or sister. They may fear that they will be hurt or possibly killed. They may also fear "catching" or having a similar issue or mental health problem.

When there is a lot going on in a family, every sibling is at risk of experiencing significant emotional distress. This does not mean they have the "same" problem as their brother or sister, but it does mean that parents, professionals, and others close to them have a responsibility to get them any help they might need.

Signs to Watch For In Your Other Children and Youth

- Extreme sadness
- Does not discuss the sibling with problems
- Excessive crying
- Avoiding the entire family or staying in their room
- Locking themselves in their room
- Grades drop at school
- Clinging or not wanting to leave parents
- Getting into trouble (possibly to get attention)
- Running away
- Changes in sleeping or eating habits
- Any behavior that concerns you

These behaviors can be a sign that siblings are struggling with what is happening to the family. Bring these behaviors to the attention of a professional who can help.

TRY THIS...

- Find ways to **ensure your other children are not feeling neglected** or guilty about what is happening. This might involve watching a few minutes of a favorite video or playing a short game of checkers.

- Many providers offer **in home services**. These may help your child feel like a part of what is happening and give them some insight into what everyone is doing about it.

- **Take your children with you** to a few appointments so they can see that their brother/sister is not having fun.

- Set up an opportunity for your children to **spend special time with someone they admire**. This can be an uncle, a neighbor, or even the coach at the school.

- Make up a game called "I Have a Secret" and **take turns telling secrets** to one another. Make some of the secrets funny, like "I secretly love spinach". Don't discuss the secrets, just reveal them. This will make them more comfortable in sharing their secrets.

- Set up a "mailbox" to **leave letters for one another**. Make some letters a simple "I love you" while others may include questions for them to answer. This is a less stressful way for you and your children or youth to talk about tough subjects.

Telling Others

"It hurt. It really hurt. I told them what was going on with Latoya. They still acted like it was something I was doing wrong. I needed their support, not their accusing finger pointing at me."

It is never easy to explain to others what is wrong with your child or youth. Emotional and mental disorders are difficult to describe to someone who is not familiar with them. Families often struggle to find the right way and time to disclose what is wrong with their child to friends, neighbors, and relatives. It is not unusual to have concerns or fears related to telling others about your child's mental or behavioral needs.

You may not feel comfortable telling others about your child's or youth's mental or behavioral needs because:

- You may not feel that you know enough about your child's or youth's condition to answer questions.

- Others may judge you since there are still many people in the world who feel that emotional and mental health disorders are the result of poor parenting and discipline.

- You may worry that some people may think you are just making excuses for your child's or youth's behavior.

- The label "mentally ill" carries a stigma, for the child or youth and the family. In the past, persons were persecuted for being mentally ill. You may fear that your child or youth will suffer at the hands of ignorant people.

- Giving a diagnosis or putting a name to what is happening means that you are acknowledging that there is a problem. Some families pretend that there is nothing wrong as a means of protecting their feelings.

There are also many reasons why families chose to share what is happening. This can include:

- When people know what you are facing, some will reach out and support you in any way they can.

- Telling others what is wrong may help reduce their judgment of you and your child or youth. Some people can identify better with a diagnosis than a behavior.

- For each person you tell, you have just educated another person about mental illness and given them a first-hand glimpse on the impact it has on families.

- By being open and honest, you are teaching your child and family that you have nothing to hide or to be embarrassed about.

What to say, how to say it, and who to tell is a personal decision. It is up to you and your family to decide when and what to tell others. Your culture, where you live, what you do for a living, and your family traditions can all influence how or if you tell others. ***If your child is old enough to understand what is happening, he or she should be consulted and have a voice in what is said, when and to whom.***

When telling other people about your child's mental disorder it is important to:

- ➢ Do it at a time and place that gives you the opportunity to share, answer questions, and have privacy. The mall or grocery stores are not good settings for this.

- ➢ Bring a fact sheet on your child's disorder to guide your answers and share information.

- ➢ Try not to read too much into comments and questions. Maybe they are not questioning what you are telling them but are trying to understand what it means so they can better support you.

- ➢ Let them know that you need their support and help. When they ask what they can do to help, give them an answer. If you do not know, let them know you just need them to listen, accept you and what your family is going through, and that you may think of something later.

> ➢ Don't spend a lot of time and emotional energy trying to convince someone of your child's diagnosis. It will wear you out and probably won't change how they feel. If it is someone close to you (a spouse or parent, for example) you might have someone else talk with them. You might also ask one of the professionals treating your child or youth to talk with them about the diagnosis and treatment. This might make them feel like a part of the team and encourage their support.

People may say things when they are told about an emotional or mental health disorder that is hurtful to the family. Below are a few suggestions on how to answer them in a way that helps them understand the issues you face.

THEY SAY: "Maybe you should just spend more time with him."
YOUR REPLY: "That is a good idea and will be a part of the special care he or she gets."

THEY SAY: "Can't you just tell him no."
YOUR REPLY: "Unfortunately, kids with this type of problem don't respond like other children. We are getting help on exactly how to handle this."

THEY SAY: "All kids this age have problems."
YOUR REPLY: "Yes, but when those problems get out of control, someone has to be willing to get extra help for them."

THEY SAY: "She is just naughty."
YOUR REPLY: "I wish it were that simple. But the doctors are helping us sort it all out."

THEY SAY: "I would never allow my child to get away with that."
YOUR REPLY: "That's what I used to say! But I am learning that an emotional or mental health disorder is not under my control. It actually takes a whole team of specialists, including us, to make sure she has the best outcome possible."

TRY THIS...

- **Take a friend or relative with you to an appointment** so they can get a firsthand look at the needs your child has above and beyond that of other children.

- Practice what you are going to say to a friend and ask for feedback. **Be prepared for misunderstandings** by people who need education on emotional and mental disorders.

- Do not do it all alone. **Ask friends and family to help** be a spokesperson for your child or youth and family. Have them go with you when you have meetings or when you tell others about your child or youth and their needs. Or, give them the information they need and let them help you inform or educate those that could help. Make sure they know who you want to have this personal information about your family.

Dealing with Stress

"All of the sudden, I was sick, too. The doctor told me if I didn't take better care of myself, I would die. I guess it hadn't hit me, what all of this with Steve was doing to me. I couldn't remember when I had spent a few minutes to myself, not thinking of what I needed to do for someone else. I thought I thrived on stress. But now I was drained and barely had the energy to climb out of the hole I was in."

The feelings and experiences of families of children or youth with emotional or mental disorders can add up to a great deal of stress. The pressure from the chaos at home, costs, loss of time at work, scheduling appointments, and other related issues can cause immense stress. It is important to recognize that stress can take a significant toll on your family and identify ways to alleviate it.

Some symptoms of stress can include:

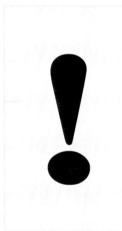

- **Dizziness**
- **Headache**
- **Stomachache**
- **Trouble sleeping or eating**
- **Frequent illness**
- **High blood pressure**
- **Others**

Learn what triggers stress in you and do everything possible to minimize its effects. Consider what stresses you the most, how you feel, and how you deal with it.

Professionals have spent a lot of time looking at how stress affects people and how to reduce its impact. Unfortunately, many of the suggestions for relieving stress are difficult for families with a child or youth who has emotional, behavioral, or mental health issues. They cannot walk away or take long, quiet evening strolls. They don't have the money to join clubs or the time to pursue outside interests. Families have become creative and learned to adapt in ways that will lower the stress levels in the home.

 **TRY THIS...**

- Make reducing stress and staying alive **a part of YOUR treatment plan**.

- Set a **certain room of your house "off limits"** to the kids (the bedroom works well). Save this as your quiet place where you are not to be disturbed except for major emergencies (be sure you spell out what an emergency is). Schedule time away and listen to YOUR music, exercise, or just close your eyes and relax.

- Get up one hour before the rest of the family and pop in your favorite movie or stand out on the porch with your favorite gourmet coffee. Just know that this is YOUR moment...**your time to prepare for the day**.

- **Celebrate** more often. These can be simple family celebrations for the end of school, good report cards, and other things beyond the typical holidays and birthdays. You can also find little known reasons for celebration such as a famous athlete's birthday, the anniversary of the day you got a family pet, or even the holiday of another country or culture.

- Know when you are on "overload" and **start cutting back**. When you hit this point, cancel unnecessary appointments, scratch activities that stress you, and don't volunteer to do ANYTHING more. Do not allow yourself to feel guilty...just say "No".

- **Get a life**!!! Find something you like to do and insist that you be allowed to have the time to do it. Have your doctor write a "prescription" and tell your family it is a must. Force yourself to take the time and energy to support your ambitions or hobbies.

WARNING! Ask yourself.....who will care for your family if you are unable to. Stress can cripple. It can significantly reduce your energy level, especially when you are stressed for a long time. It can rob you of what little joy you may have in your life! Stress can kill. **Talk to your doctor or another professional** about how you can reduce stress in your life.

Preventing Drop Out

"I am tired of it all. My way of coping has been an "I no longer care anymore" attitude. I just feel like I have tried for so many years to do the right things, to get people to believe me. Now, with the diagnosis in, I am so full of resentment and bitterness, I just don't care. Tired is what I am, tired of doing it all, tired of watching the time go by, tired of knowing that as time passes, so does his chances, tired of explaining, tracking, arguing, defending...."

Families of children and youth with emotional or mental health disorders are often overwhelmed by their situation and experiences. Sometimes it becomes so overwhelming that they "drop out" of their child's or youth's life. When a family loses hope, when they are robbed of their dignity, when they no longer can trust one another; dropping out becomes their way out and a way to protect their already damaged feelings. Many of us have been very close to dropping out as our child's primary caretaker. Sometimes the pain is too much and the road seems too long; letting the child or youth go....to the state, to the streets, or to nowhere might seem like the only answer. We may be ready to get it over and reach what we have been told is the inevitable outcome; "He will end up in jail", "She will run away someday and never come back" or "He will probably get so depressed we will not be able to stop a suicide attempt." The predictions we have heard become the expectation...they become what we have to look forward to. The important thing is to keep yourself from getting to that point.

WARNING SIGNS OF THE DROP OUT PARENT
- A feeling that nothing will ever change your child or youth
- No longer attending meetings or appointments for your child
- Feeling that your child or youth would be better off without you
- Feeling that you would be better off without your child or youth
- No longer discussing how your child or youth is doing with professionals
- A lack of interest in how your child or youth is progressing
- Not asking your child or youth questions about school, friends, etc.

- Allowing others to make all of the decisions for your child's or youth's needs
- Not returning phone calls concerning your child or youth
- Not reading mail or letters concerning your child or youth

While many of these feelings happen to everyone at some time or another, they may be a sign that you are starting to pull away from your child and wish to drop out as a parent. Wanting to drop out is perfectly understandable but this is a thought that should come and go; not stay around for days at a time. Dropping out is a way of protecting yourself and your feelings. It is a side effect of exhaustion and ongoing stress. With the appropriate supports, you can continue to be a major player in your child's or youth's life and be the difference in their future success and independence.

 **TRY THIS...**

- One of the best ways to not drop out of your child's or youth's life is to **make sure you have a life beyond them** as well. Sometimes it seems impossible, but given the alternatives, it is important. You need a reason to go on, a purpose bigger than one family member, and something that is not related to all of the energy draining activities that seem to rule your life.

- Participate in **activities that are yours alone**, such as exercising or sewing.

- Accept your limits on what and how much you can do. Make a **list of what you will not do**...like "I don't wash windows".

- Learn to **expect the unexpected** and plan for it. Make a real disaster plan based upon the kind of disasters your family has to face.

- **Take care of yourself**, exercise, keep fit, and eat right.

- **Have some friends who do not have children with special needs** and practice just being a parent of your child or youth, not the parent of a child or youth with mental health care needs.

- Start a collection of inspirational quotes. You might enjoy **creating a quote scrapbook** where you can retreat regularly for an emotional "recharge".

- **Join the sports craze**....pick a team, buy a T-shirt, and set game day aside as your time to retreat from the real world.

- **Divide responsibilities** for your child or youth with others. They do not need to be family and the only requirement is that they are willing to help. Someone else can go to the school open house conference this year. Allow someone else the privilege of taking your child or youth to an appointment. Trade with them things they dread, like washing windows, shopping, or washing the car.

Notes

Finding Support, Help, and Relief

"Sometimes I just needed a break...a break from the constant vigilance, the worry, the reminders that our lives have all changed"

You will find that from time to time you will need some support. You might get the support you need by accessing information. Sometimes the informal supports you get from family and friends may adequately address your needs, while at other times you may need a formal system of organized support. This section looks at various types of support and services available and resources that might help families and their children and youth.

Support Groups

"I felt so alone. When I started to meet other families that had a child like Tara, I started to live again. I had put my feelings on hold for a long time. I never knew who to share with; how much they could understand. Now, I can just say what I mean, and I know I am not the only one who feels that way."

Many families feel alone when they have a child or youth with special needs. You may live in a world where those around you have never had to have their child hospitalized or had a call in the middle of the night from the police. They may not know what it is like to go through a series of evaluations to learn why their child or youth cannot manage their behavior. Few parents have had to go to the school to pick up their child or youth because he or she has been expelled for behavior issues. During group conversations, people tend to talk about politics, current events, or happy family outings. As the parent of a child or youth with an emotional, behavioral, or mental health disorder, you are more concerned about how you will get through the night; if your child or youth will be allowed on the school bus; or how you will get everyone to eat together at the table tonight.

Self-help or support groups bring together people with common situations to share resources, support, and ideas. They serve as a means of supporting one another based on the "I've been there" approach. Sometimes they are called peer to peer groups; or families helping families. Some support groups are very formal, with elected leadership and an agenda for each meeting. These groups may have featured speakers or a meeting theme that concentrates on a particular topic, like how to get respite. Other groups are very informal and are a time for sharing stories, experiences, and concerns. Self-help or support groups may use a professional as the facilitator or may have members take turns leading each session. Support groups may be offered through a school, church, program, agency, or other community group.

You your family and your child or youth can get support in many ways. There are organized efforts to connect families of children with special needs in every state in the nation. There are also state and national conferences that focus on how to help families support one another. And most local agencies and service programs recognize the need for families to share and support one another. There are also support groups and conferences just for youth.

Benefits of a Support
- Spending time with others who understand
- Not having to worry about being judged
- Sharing experiences and hearing about what worked for other families
- Finding out you are not alone
- Using a group approach for solving problems

Support Options for Families

Support Parents
Support Parents are trained to act as a support for other families. They are usually the parent of a child or youth with a mental health disorder who has several years of experience working with their child, service providers, and the system. They know how to listen and assist you in finding ways to manage the daily frustrations related to your child's or youth's disorder. They also build a friendship that allows an open sharing of common experiences without judgment or interference. You may first meet a support parent at a treatment center or from home by telephone but support parent programs may also include home visits.

Support Group Meetings
Families of children and youth with similar diagnoses may meet on a regular basis to share frustrations, joys, and celebrate their accomplishments. Special speakers or professionals come in to talk about issues of concern and to answer questions. This informal atmosphere allows you to get information while supported by other families who understand.

Newsletters
Many families wish to receive support and information, but do not want to participate in meetings or share in an open forum. Reading

newsletters can be an excellent way to get information and know that you are not alone, in the comfort and privacy of your own home. Newsletters provide information, resources, and an opportunity to learn about families such as yours.

Websites, Blogs, and Social Marketing Groups
Many websites have information and resources for families of children and youth with emotional, behavioral, or mental health disorders. These websites may provide a way to blog (share your views, stories, or discuss your views via an internet discussion board), to leave messages, have discussions with other families or professionals, or get the names and contact information for resources or support activities in your community. Many social marketing sites such as Face Book offer families an internet community where they can share celebrations, frustrations, and ideas.

Conferences
Most mental health and disability organizations have annual conferences where members gather for workshops, support sessions, and sharing information. You may find this an excellent "respite" for getting away while learning more about your child's or youth's problems and alternative treatments. These are usually expensive, but organizations often have stipends or scholarships for parents and family members.

Disability and Mental Health Organizations
There are thousands of state and national organizations in the US that have membership focused upon a certain disability or mental health conditions. They typically offer many of the support services listed above and also work to give voice to your concerns at a political level; assuring that children and youth with special needs do not go unrecognized during periods of reform and change. You may find that joining their efforts gives you a new "reason" to go on; helping others to transform the system and make it more responsive to other families with similar issues and needs.

While many families enjoy the support they find through groups, meetings, and organizations, many do not. If you feel that you would like to learn more about what supports might be available for you, look at the information included in the Resource Section. Try a few options and see if it is something you enjoy or feel makes your role as a parent easier. There is no long-term commitment and you can feel comfortable not continuing to participate if it is not right for you.

TRY THIS...

- **Ask** one of your child's or youth's providers or the school if there is a support group in your area. If there is not, look on the internet for options in your area.

- Ask the school to **sponsor a "support and information fair"** where service providers, agencies, and programs can set up booths and display information. They also have professionals available to answer questions. Information concerning children's mental illness is displayed and can be picked up by families that attend. Support organizations attend with representative to explain how their membership works and the benefits to families. You can assist in the planning and ensure that parents of children and youth with mental and emotional disorders from around the area as well other professionals, programs, and agencies are invited.

- **Start your own** Face Book page for families of children and youth with emotional, behavioral, and mental health disorders. Add links to resources and other pages and post about some of the issues and challenges you and other families face.

Respite Care

Meeting the needs of your child or youth with an emotional, behavioral, or mental health disorder can be very difficult and drain you of energy and strength. Respite care is the temporary care of a person with special needs to allow parents or other caregivers a break. Respite care provides the short term breaks that can relieve stress, restore energy, and promote balance in your life.

As discussed in more detail below, there are many ways in which respite care can be provided. It can be provided in the child's or youth's home or may be provided in a location where your child or youth will stay for a short period of time. Some families make informal respite care arrangements, such as having other family members, neighbors, or friends watch their child or youth for a short period of time. Family members and friends may be able to help out while you run an errand or take a break. Some families access respite through one of their providers or a community program. Since families have different needs, respite care should be specially tailored to each family and their child or youth. Arranging to get respite from family members or friends can be difficult, but there may be more formal respite care options and strategies that can offer you and your family a needed break.

IN-HOME OR COMMUNITY RESPITE
Sitter, Mentor or Companion services
A sitter or companion is an individual who may be specially trained to care for a child or youth who experiences emotional or mental health disorders. These individuals spend time working on specific activities that help teach your child or youth new skills in overcoming the effects of their disorder. In-home respite can be provided by volunteer or paid help, depending on your resources and the programs that support you and your child or youth. In home respite allows your children and youth to remain in their own environments, and may occur on a regular basis or as needed.

Friends, Neighbors, and other Families
Creative parents and caregivers may take turns watching each other's children, giving and taking breaks when needed. You may "swap" time with another parent or friend; allowing a friend or family member

come to your home to stay with your child or youth for a short period and later returning the favor.

OUT OF HOME RESPITE

Care in a Provider's Home

Arrangements can be made for your child or youth to go to a sitter's or companion's home for care for a period of time. You might use this option to take a weekend break or a short vacation. You may also opt to trade time with someone else; sending your child or youth with another family for a brief period and taking their child or youth in return.

Group day care

Group day care is a program in which children and youth with emotional, behavioral, and mental health disorders go for the day to participate in activities that builds their skills under professional supervision. You may choose to leave your child or youth at a center with specially trained staff that can provide constant and regular services throughout the week.

Residential respite care

Residential respite care allows your child or youth to stay with other children and youth with similar disorders in a home that is designed especially for respite and uses trained staff that works in shifts. The length of time in care can range from a weekend to a month or more, depending on your program or service eligibility.

Residential treatment respite services

Some treatment facilities, like hospitals or residential centers reserve a few places ("beds") for their respite service programs. This type of respite may be especially helpful for you if your child or youth has severe problems that require around the clock care. Residential treatment respite has back up with well-trained staff and medical professionals that are always available, but the cost is usually high.

Crisis & Emergency Respite Care Facilities

Crisis and emergency respite services are for families who are temporarily unable to care for their child or youth. These facilities focus on the family's immediate need to provide care for your child or youth facing a crisis or emergency. Examples include the illness or death of an immediate family member; a crisis at home that makes caring for your child or youth impossible, or other situation which would make it difficult to keep your child or youth at home. Some residential care facilities provide emergency respite care on a limited basis.

OTHER FORMS OF HOME AND COMMUNITY BASED RESPITE

Respite comes as a side benefit of other programs such as school, camp, after-school activities, vacation Bible School, organized sports, and other group activities. Many conferences for families offer on-site youth groups and respite care so you can attend sessions and take part in activities while your children and youth are kept busy with their peers. These all give you a short break and provide supervision, support, and fun activities for your child or youth on a regular and predictable basis.

BENEFITS OF RESPITE CARE

- ➢ Allows your child or youth to be with others outside of your family
- ➢ Prevents burnout or exhaustion
- ➢ Encourages the family to socialize without your child or youth with mental disorders
- ➢ Gives you time to spend with your other children
- ➢ Allows you to attend other appointments (like going to see *your* doctor)
- ➢ Helps build your child's or youth's independence
- ➢ Helps maintain your own physical health
- ➢ Allows your family to have experiences like other families

THINGS TO CONSIDER

- ☑ Payment for respite services
- ☑ Training of respite providers
- ☑ Your family's involvement in developing the plan of care
- ☑ Consistency in the care of your child or youth

HOW YOU CAN HELP MAKE RESPITE WORK FOR YOUR FAMILY

Be open about your child's or youth's needs.
Keep everyone up to date on your child's or youth's needs so that they can better appreciate the work it takes and they can better understand how they can help.

Ask family and friends to help.
Share your list of needs and take advantage of all offers to help.

Organize your needs and solicit help.
Consider establishing an online calendar that shows when help is needed and allow family and friends to choose when they can assist.

Use the internet to help keep others up to date.
Participate in a web-based community to share updates and help others understand what is happening with your child or youth. Take advantage of sites like carepages.com to keep family and friends up-to-date and in touch.

Start a respite cooperative.
Trade respite services with other caregivers and their families, taking turns and sharing in the care and offering short periods of respite.

SELECTING A RESPITE PROGRAM FOR YOUR CHILD OR YOUTH

Selecting a person or program to care for your child or youth is a serious decision. To help ensure the safety of your child or youth, make sure you:

- Interview the program or individuals who will be providing care.
- If a first interview is done by phone, follow up with a face-to-face interview.
- Be specific about your child's or youth's needs, treatment, and schedules.
- Visit the location where respite services will be provided.
- Discuss how and when payment for respite will occur.
- Request several work *and* personal references and check them carefully.
- Verify all information and references, and ask about reliability, trustworthiness, punctuality and the care provider's ability to handle stress.
- If you are selecting and paying a person to provide respite directly (not through a program or agency) you should consider a

background check. Check with your local police department, legal aid service or attorney for referrals to reputable investigators or search for "background checks" on the Internet.

▪ Ask for the names of other families that have been in the program or that received respite from the provider. Call and ask about the quality of care they received and if there were any problems you should be aware of.

When using a respite program through an agency you might ask:
- ❏ How are respite providers screened?
- ❏ What is the required training and level of experience of their providers?
- ❏ Will care providers need additional training to meet your child's or youth's needs?
- ❏ Who supervises providers and how is this done?
- ❏ What happens if there is an emergency?
- ❏ How am I notified it there is an emergency?
- ❏ If my child needs immediate medical care, to what hospital would he or she be taken?
- ❏ Can we visit the program or facility any time we wish?
- ❏ Do you provide transportation, meals, and snacks?
- ❏ What is the cost of services? How is payment arranged?

Summer Camps or other Special Programs

Summer camps and other programs for children or youth with emotional or mental health disorders are for a specified period of time during which the child resides at the location and participates in activities with other children or youth, often with similar mental health issues. Some camps or programs have a theme, such as marine science or wagon trains. Your child or youth spends time participating in activities with specially trained counselors and receives individual attention and therapy to address targeted issues.

THINGS TO CONSIDER
- ✓ The program's capacity to meet your child or youths needs
- ✓ The ability to administer medication or continue treatments currently in place
- ✓ Visitation policies
- ✓ Discipline practices
- ✓ Staff qualifications and capacity
- ✓ What programs and activities are offered that will appeal to your child or youth

When looking for a summer camp or other specialized program you should:
- Visit the program and take a tour of the facilities.
- Meet and talk with staff.
- Ask the following:
  - ❑ How are camp staff screened and hired?
  - ❑ What are the staff's qualifications?
  - ❑ Will the camp provide additional training to meet our child's or youth's needs?
  - ❑ Who supervises staff and how is this done?
  - ❑ What happens if there is an emergency?
  - ❑ How am I notified it there is an emergency?
  - ❑ If my child needs immediate medical care, to what hospital would he or she be taken?
  - ❑ Can we visit the program or camp any time we wish?
  - ❑ Do you provide all transportation, meals, and snacks?
  - ❑ Who administers medication?
  - ❑ What is the cost?

- Make sure you understand who will supervise your child or youth and how this will be done. (For example, how many campers are supervised by one staff person?)
- Provide as much medical, psychiatric, and family information as possible so they fully understand your child's or youth's needs.
- Speak with other families that have used the same program and ask what kind of experiences they had.

Roles and Opportunities

"A big part of it is not always knowing what to do. I want to be a part of my child's care, but it isn't easy. I have to learn everything about Dion's care, not just a part, but all of it. I don't have a special field; I'm responsible for the whole thing."

Your family may find itself trying to make adjustments not only to the changes in your child or youth, but also to the new responsibility that goes with having a child with special needs. You are learning a new language, taking part in planning meetings, and making life changing decisions that affect your whole family. This section is designed to help you understand your new roles and ways to find ways of doing what needs to be done as easily and effectively as possible.

Teamwork, Partnership and Collaboration

"It was so amazing. I felt so alone, but there they all were, every one of them. There was Drew's teacher, his therapist, the case manager, the probation officer, and even his coach. We were alone until we came together....then we were a team. We succeeded as a team, and when Drew fell behind, we grieved as a team."

Most children and youth with special needs will benefit from a team of experts. Everyone on the team such as a therapist, a doctor, a case manager, or a teacher has a special expertise. You are also a member of this team since you are the expert on your family. Your participation is crucial.

To make the team more successful, they partner and collaborate. Collaboration means that all members work together with the common goal of meeting your child's or youth's special needs in a way that offers the greatest chance of success. Collaboration may not always come easy because different people may have different ideas on what is best.

REMEMBER: Collaboration does not mean that everyone has to agree. It does mean that differences are addressed in a way that assures that all decisions are in the best interest of the child or youth and the family. When "what is in the best interest" is the point of disagreement, then everyone must be willing to compromise and give up some of personal beliefs and try new ideas.

Areas of Collaboration and Teamwork	How You can Use It to help Your Child or Youth and Family
Expect differences Team members will look at the issues and needs of your child or youth from a different view. Expect them to have different ideas on the most important issues and the best solutions.	Different ideas can generate new approaches and finding help that you have not had in the past.
Respect for other team members It is important to respect the ideas of other team members, even if they are different from yours.	Showing respect will earn you respect. Even when you are frustrated you will find that being respectful of other members will help assure that others respect you.
Effective listening Make sure you listen to all that is said before making a decision. Listening is not the same as agreeing and your job is to "hear" everything that is being said then make a decision that is in the best interest of your child and family.	When you listen you learn. What you learn today may not be used or needed right away but you may need it later.
More ways than one Recognize that there can be more than one good answer. There may be several different ways to approach the needs of your child and family. Because the needs of your family may be complicated, there may be no single best way to approach addressing those needs.	You already know that there are no easy answers, or you wouldn't be working with a team. Keep track of different approaches and learn what you can to help in the future.
Share abilities and resources One of the great benefits of collaboration is combining the skills and abilities of the team members into one huge resource for your family.	Participating on the team can help you feel less alone. You may feel renewed hope or a sense of power.

Shared decision making
The team will make decisions based upon the ideas that everyone has contributed. If the plan does not work, the entire team is responsible for coming up with a better approach.

When collaboration is effective, you won't feel alone because decisions are made as a team, and the team shares the responsibilities for their decisions.

Clear communication
Collaboration will require you to communicate as clearly as you can. It will not work if you hide your feelings and concerns from the rest of the team.

When working as a team there is often little time for "getting to know one another". Strong communication skills will help you be heard and ensure your ideas are considered when making decisions.

Everyone equally responsible
When you are part your child's or youth's team, you are an equal partner in the collaboration process.

Not only are you responsible to the team, they are also responsible to you, your child or youth, and your family.

Are YOU a Good Team Member?

- ☑ Can you listen to and really hear members who have ideas that differ from yours?
- ☑ Are you able to speak about your child or youth and family needs?
- ☑ Are you willing to meet with all of your child's team, even those with whom you disagree?
- ☑ Can you share your ideas and concerns with the team?
- ☑ Will you listen to and really hear everyone's ideas before making a decision on what is best for your child or youth?
- ☑ Can you explain your views without getting angry or blaming others?
- ☑ Are you willing to try new ideas to help your child or youth?
- ☑ Do you feel that your child or youth needs more help than you can give?

*The more times you can answer "yes" to the questions above, the better your chances are of becoming an effective team member.

 **TRY THIS...**

- **Call on the "team"** and bring them together to discuss ideas, share solutions, and discuss frustrations. This will help everyone meet and know each other and set a foundation for working as a team in the future.

- Let others know when a team member does something that works out especially well. **Complement others** with notes, praise, and "warm fuzzies" for the good that is done for your child or youth.

- Make your team a part of your child's or youth's successes. **Include them in celebrations** such as birthdays, graduations, or other milestones.

- Start each meeting of the team with a celebration of some success, no matter how small. This helps them **keep in touch with the personal side of your child, youth, or family** and makes them feel a part of all accomplishments.

Family Driven Care

"It is my kid they are talking about. I have to live with these decisions forever. He will live with these decisions forever."

Being a member of the team and collaborating does not mean that you give up your role as the person responsible for your child or youth. The mental health field uses the term "family driven; youth guided" to describe an approach that includes families, consumers, providers, and programs collaborating at various levels of service planning, delivery, and implementation. *Family-driven means families have a primary decision making role in the care of their own children as well as the policies and procedures governing care for all children in their community, state, tribe, territory and nation.* This includes:

1. Choosing supports, services, and providers for their child or youth;
2. Setting goals for their child, youth, or family;
3. Helping design and implement mental health programs and services;
4. Monitoring outcomes and helping decide if they were successful;
5. Partnering in deciding how money for mental health programs are spent

(Adapted from: Osher, T and Blau, G. 2007. Gaithersburg, MD: Federation of Families for Children's Mental Health and Center for Mental Health Services, Substance Abuse and Mental Health Services Administration)

Making Family Driven Work for You

Know what you want for your child or youth	You need to know how you want things to be in order to move forward from where you are now and set goals for the future.
Know how to explain what your child or youth needs	You may need to practice explaining what you need for your child or youth. If you really want to get help, it is critical that you can talk about what you need in a way that others can understand
Learn all you can about your child's or youth's condition	The more you know the better you can understand what may or may not assist your child or youth.

Take your role on the team seriously	In a family driven world, families are the drivers of the team. You are the most important member of the team. If you want to be taken seriously and be respected in that role, you need to accept the responsibility of being the leader and act the part.
Know the role of others on your child's or youth's team and what they can and cannot do	It is easier to get assistance from others when you know what they can do to help you. This ensures that you do not waste time asking for help from the wrong person or resource.
Understand the children's mental health system in your state and community	The mental health system is not perfect. Change will only happen through the involvement of families that have lived through the successes and failures of the system and know what it takes to meet the real needs of families like themselves.

 # TRY THIS...

- **Educate others** on your child's or youth's team about the concept of "family driven" and discuss how you can make sure that your services are family driven.

- Contact a family run and/or an advocacy organization and ask them to **set up a training session on family driven care** in your community. Invite the members of your child's or youth's team and attend with them.

- When professionals respond to you, your child or youth, or other families in a family driven manner, **give them recognition**. You might create a "Family Driven Recognition Award" or a "Family Driven Hall of Fame" at conferences or in newsletters.

Expressing Yourself

"They wanted to know what I thought and all I could do was cry. I had a chance to share with them what we needed, and all I did was cry. They were very understanding, but I wish I had better control of myself."

When your child has special needs, it is more important than ever to be able to speak clearly and help others understand what you need. Many families are overwhelmed with the feelings, chaos, and new demands that they face each day. Anytime you are dealing with issues that are emotional, it is important that you communicate as clearly as possible. Describing your child's or youth's needs and sharing experiences can take a heavy emotional toll on you and your family. However, communicating clearly can be one of the best ways of getting the services your child needs.

You will be asked over and over again to talk about what is happening with your child or youth. There are so many things to deal with when you are trying to communicate. Some of these might include:
- Getting people to understand what your child or youth needs
- Getting others to understand how they can help your family
- Sharing information about the struggles you are having
- Making your feelings understood
- Making a point or disagreeing with team members
- Standing up for your child's or youth's rights
- Asking questions about services, treatments, or programs
- Telling others about your child's or youth's special needs

Because communication is much more than just the words that you say, you may be communicating more about your situation than you realize. Below are examples of ways you communicate through your actions and your words.
- What you say
- The tone of your voice
- Your body language (how you hold your body)
- Where you sit
- Where you look

Many people don't realize that it is often what they <u>don't say</u> that says the most. Professionals may count heavily on what you say to them, but they may also be watching for other communication clues. Most professionals take several classes in college that focus on communication; how to talk, how to listen, and how to interpret what people say. You may be telling them more than you know:

Nonverbal Communication Cue	What It MAY Mean to Others
Crossed arms	You disagree with someone or something or are angry and do not want to be there
Clearing throat	You would like a turn to talk
Sitting at the head of the table	You are confident and feel in control
Talking softly	You are not sure about what you are saying
Avoiding eye contact	You are avoiding the truth or are unsure of yourself
Playing with hands	You are bored, not interested, or are done with this conversation and ready to move on

Some simple and easy to remember suggestions for communicating more clearly and effectively include:
- Speak clearly and speak in the language that is most comfortable for you.
- Look at the people with whom you are talking.
- Repeat what you have already said if you think this will help others understand what you are saying.
- Ask if you are being clear of if you need to explain something in a different way.
- If you need to pause, say that you need a few seconds...no need to apologize.

- Ask someone you trust to come with you to help you remember the important points you want to make.
- Write down the most important points you want to make on a piece of paper, which you can refer to while you are talking; but don't write out a speech.
- Try to make one or two points at a time, rather than explaining everything at once. This allows others to ask questions about things that they don't understand.
- Remember that others may not agree with what you are saying even when you have communicated in a clear and effective manner.

You may be concerned about how you communicate. Following are a few things that might make you nervous about communicating with others regarding the mental or behavioral needs of your child or youth.

I might cry or show some other emotion.	It is important that you do not misunderstand the role emotions play in communication. Some emotions are hard to hide. Culture, family traditions, and past experiences all impact how and where you show your emotions.
I may say or do the wrong thing and they will judge me for it.	Try to stay focused on the outcome you would like for your child or youth. Use that as your guide and remember that making progress toward that outcome is what counts the most.
I am just a parent, I do not know anything.	You are the expert on your child or youth and your family. What you have to say will help everyone understand the situation and identify what can help the most.
I cannot speak well or use big words like the professionals.	Be open and honest and try to be yourself, not someone else. Use the words that you understand and repeat yourself several times if others do seem to understand what you are saying.

TRY THIS...

- Try taking in front of the mirror and "discussing" several issues that are important to you. This REALLY can help you feel more confident and **build your speaking skills**.

- Rehearse making your point with a friend; convince them of something, ask for something, and disagree on an issue. **Ask for help and feedback** on how you can be more convincing.

- **Watch someone** you admire communicate. It could be the President, a teacher, or an actor. Notice the tone of their voice, how they hold their hands, and what they do with their head.

Your Child's Advocate:

"Here I am, in the middle of a room full of people who all think they know what it best for Jess. They don't have a clue! What they are asking is impossible and won't make the difference they think it will. What we really need is an after school program for her. She requires structure and a rigid schedule."

An advocate is a person who speaks on behalf of someone who cannot speak for themselves. There is no one better to speak on behalf of your child or youth than you. As a parent or family member, you know your child or youth best. You have a good idea about how this disorder impacts your family. You know the world your child or youth lives in beyond the doors of the hospital, clinic, or school halls. You understand your family traditions and culture in a way that no one else does. Years from now, you will be the one who will have to answer questions about the decisions that were made. The professionals will have moved onto other patients or clients.

Because you are so important to your child or youth, it is vital that you develop the skills you need to advocate in the most effective ways possible. How well you speak up for your child or youth can make a big difference in the services, treatment, and programs he or she will receive.

A GOOD ADVOCATE IS ONE WHO...
- Respects the roles and responsibilities of all team members
- Knows the rights of children and youth with mental health issues
- Can speak clearly about the child, youth, and family needs
- Focuses on the child and family, not the disorder
- Spends the time necessary for others to really understand the issues
- Listens to all points of view
- Knows what services and providers work well
- Keeps a list of contacts, phone calls, and notes on appointments and meetings
- Follows through on all commitments or gets assistance to be sure they get done

Advocacy does not mean that you always get your way or that you always make everyone else agree with you. Rather, it means that your interactions with professionals always focus on achieving what you feel is in the best interest of your child or youth. You are there to help guide decisions and to protect the rights of your child or youth and family.

STEPS TO EFFECTIVE ADVOCACY

1. Know your child or youth and their mental health or behavioral needs and how it may impact their lives, ability to learn, and opportunity for a successful future.
2. Find out all you can about the services, agencies, and programs serving your child or youth and family.
3. Gather information, listen to others, and learn about options before advocating on an issue.
4. Listen to everyone involved to ensure you have accurate, current and complete information.
5. Don't argue. State your concerns and ideas clearly and with an expectation that those concerns will be resolved.
6. Stand firm on what you believe is necessary for your child or youth.
7. Go from one level to another and utilize any and all resources available to get what you feel you must have for your child or youth.
8. When you are not sure about what to do or say, don't do or say anything (under react). Ask for a break or reschedule the meeting so you have time to think and then react.
9. Try to always have a positive and non-judgmental attitude about resolving the issue.
10. Treat everyone as you would hope someone would treat you in the same situation.
11. Make sure that everyone understands what is expected of them.
12. Let everyone know that you feel responsible for making things work out for your child or youth.
13. Follow your discussions/decisions with a letter highlighting what you understood and mail by registered letter to ensure it arrived. You may also send an email with a confirmation receipt.

TRY THIS...

- Look for ways to **have others join in on your efforts**. Teachers or others close to your child or youth are often excellent advocates. Ask them to personally assist you and offer them the opportunity to help.

- Learn **how you advocate best**. If it is through talking, then advocate in person. If you write moving letters, use that as your approach.

- When something is very serious and **you do not want it overlooked**, send a certified letter stating your concerns. Do this only for critical situations. If you do this too often, professionals will feel that you over-react and may pay less attention to your requests.

- **Get training** from a group or organization on how to advocate for your child or youth. Look for those organizations that provide resources and support after the training, so you can get the additional help you may need to be successful.

- Once you have become an advocate for your own child or youth, you may be interested in **advocating for better services for all children and youth** with mental health needs. There are many groups of families and other interested persons who are working to change the system and make it more responsive to the needs of children and youth and their families.

Keeping Track

"There were pieces of Doug's life at one hospital and more in another. Each therapist kept their own records. Then the school had some records and so did the mental health center. If I didn't keep up with our own set of records, there is no way anyone could possibly know where to gather it all up."

When your child or youth is receiving services over a long period of time or from several different providers, keeping track of it all can become a nightmare. Each professional or program that has contact with your child or youth will start its own file. Some professionals/programs will keep a few pieces of information in their file and might not share this information with others. However, every small piece of information is important and necessary in assembling an accurate and comprehensive understanding of your child or youth and family. Tests may be repeated unnecessarily or your child or youth may be examined by the same type of specialist twice because results of previous tests cannot be located. As a parent or caregiver, you are in an excellent position to keep your own copy of your child's or youth's records. When your child becomes an adult, this comprehensive health record is something you will be able to pass this on, since he or she will need it for managing their own health care. And since they will have to maintain this record when they are an adult, think about teaching them how to do this when they are in their teens.

| *Start with what you already have.* | *Begin immediately to add each report, evaluation, or test as it is completed.* | *Gradually add to this with past reports, appointments, tests, and other recorded information.* |

Record Keeping Tips
- Use file folders or loose leaf binders
- Make sections or folders for each of the main types of services your child or youth receives, such as
  - ✓ School
  - ✓ Hospitalizations
  - ✓ Medicaid
  - ✓ Family Service or Care Management Plans
  - ✓ Therapy
  - ✓ Insurance
  - ✓ Case Management
  - ✓
- Whenever a service is provided, request a copy of the summary to put in the file.
- Ask providers to put recommendations or progress in a "6-month report" and add these reports to the file regularly.
- Request a discharge summary after every hospitalization.
- Keep and file a copy of every plan, such as the IEP, 504 plan, or transition plan
- Keep a copy of school report cards and progress reports.
- Request a list of all medications your child is taking from your pharmacy or download from the pharmacy website every 3 months.
- Keep a copy of all correspondence from funding sources, like Medicaid or insurance.
- Keep the files in order by date for each type of service.
- Never give or mail YOUR copy to anyone else; request that they make a copy of what they need and return the original to you while you wait.
- As he or she grows, let your child or youth assist in maintaining these records so that she or he will understand their importance and know how to navigate the records to access necessary information.

Getting Copies of Records
When you are requesting a copy of your child's records, it may require a "release of information" form. Providers generally have their own release forms for you to sign indicating you want a copy of your child's or youth's records. These forms are filled out to indicate who is requesting the information and what and when it was given to them. This is for your child's protection and is required by law. It ensures that your child's

records are not released to anyone without your permission. This is called confidentiality.

Even with the proper permissions, some professionals are reluctant to give families copies of their child's or youth's records. This may be due to a variety of reasons including professional opinion that:

- Families may lose the records and the information will get into the wrong hands;
- Families won't understand what the records say;
- The records belong to the provider, not the family; or
- Families have no business maintaining their child's or youth's records.

Let professionals know that you keep a copy of all records pertaining to your child or youth and that you appreciate their help in keeping the master file complete. Remind them that this file could be of benefit to them when they need information that seems to be missing. You might discuss with them how important the records will be for your youth when they transition into adult health care. If you start doing this as a part of your regular collaboration routine rather than when you need records due to a conflict, it will seem less threatening.

 TRY THIS...

- Ask a professional with whom you trust to **assist you in setting up a record keeping system** for your child or youth. They may have ideas on where to start as well as release forms that will be needed to get copies from other professionals. They can show you how their records are set up and share tips on keeping them updated.

- Use an inexpensive calendar that fits into your purse or pocket or use the calendar on your cell phone or computer to **keep track of appointments, medication changes, behaviors, blood levels, and other important data**. Using a calendar in this way makes it much easier to answer questions concerning your child. You will have immediate access to dates, times, doses, medications, doctors names, etc. When asked a question like "When was the last time he had this type of behavior problem?" you can look it up and state the last day and time it occurred, rather than a vague "I think it was three weeks ago."

Notes

Helping Your Child or Youth Reach Their Potential

"If I believed what I was told, I wouldn't have expected anything out of her. She would have lived up to everyone's expectations. But we never gave up, and here we are five years later...her with a college education and a job and us still sane and intact."

All children and youth have dreams and potential; but some may need extra help in uncovering those dreams and that potential. Your child or youth with an emotional or mental health disorder will need your help and assistance as well as that of many other people to assure he or she has real opportunities to become a productive and independent adult. Your children or youth will need your support and guidance to help them in their journey towards gaining control over their behavioral and emotional problems and reaching their dreams. This section will address areas where your role and support is essential.

Your Child or Youth and Friends

> *"When he started the 6th grade he didn't have a single friend. Everyone hated him and the way he acted. I think some of them were even told by their parents to stay away from him. But, in the middle of the year this new kid came into the school. He was in the eighth grade and he put up with most of David's acting out. And he didn't have any anger at David, because he never knew him before. Emory did more for David that year than any of his therapy."*

Friends are an important part of growing up. Children learn about the world around them and their place in it through their friendships. As children grow into adolescence, friends become their world...they become the center of their life. But, when a child is living with an emotional or mental disorder, getting and keeping friends can be difficult. As a parent, you will probably go back and forth between wanting your child or youth to have friendships and worry that friendships will mean more work for you; supervision, refereeing fights, explaining behaviors to other parents, and the constant fear that an argument could leave both your child or youth and his friend devastated.

There are a variety of things that you can do to help foster your child's or youth's friendships. Here are a few:
- ❖ Make your home a welcome place for your child or youth and his or her friends
- ❖ Offer to car pool other children to and from school or other activities
- ❖ Become a sports coach
- ❖ Volunteer at school where you can encourage and monitor friendships
- ❖ Get involved in a place of worship
- ❖ Invite families to your home for celebrations, picnics, or other activity
- ❖ Begin an after school-play group

Your role in helping your child or youth to make and keep friends is limited. You can set the stage, but the rest is up to them. You should try to teach and reinforce the qualities other people find attractive in a friend. Be a good role model for your child or youth and talk often about the qualities that make a good friend. When you see them being a good friend, compliment them.

Families can help by reminding children and youth that to be a good friend they must:
- ✓ Respect the belongings of their friends
- ✓ Listen and not interrupt others when they speak
- ✓ Not hurt other people
- ✓ Not call other people names
- ✓ Not say bad things about their friends to others
- ✓ Share with friends
- ✓ Take turns and sometimes do things their friends want to do
- ✓ Apologize and feel sorry for doing something wrong
- ✓ Not embarrass their friends in public or tease them

REMEMBER:

You must be careful that your child or youth are not hurt by artificial friendships. Children and youth with special needs can be the target of people with problems of their own and possibly dangerous motives. Discuss such things as sex abuse, drugs, alcohol, bullying, and risk taking with your child or youth. Review these concerns with them often and support their decisions to stay away from certain children and youth.

 **TRY THIS...**

- Look for an older child or youth as a **friend for your child**. They are often more tolerant and understanding of special problems. Friends do not have to be the same age.

- Ask the teacher to **help foster friendships**. They usually know who has the personality and maturity to be a good friend for your child or youth.

- Make **friends with other people** who have children and youth. Your children can learn a lot from watching you as a role model. They may be a little timid at first in a new or unfamiliar situation, but when they see you interacting with others, they may follow your footsteps.

Fostering Self-Confidence

"I could tell by her face that the others kids had picked on her. As she got into the car and started to sob, I couldn't help but hate them. I know that she deserves some of what she gets, but she really can't help it and they can. I feel so bad..."

Children and youth with mental, behavioral, or emotional disorders often do not feel good about themselves. Your child or youth may have heard others talk about how "bad" they are. They may have lost friends and been called names by their peers. They may want to be like everyone else, but cannot manage to do so because of their disorder. Children and youth with low self-confidence may do poorly in school, struggle in relationships, and have problems managing their behaviors. Because low self-esteem is so common with children and youth who have emotional and mental disorders, it is important to create new ways of making them feel accepted.

We all remember how mean other children and youth can be. Most of us shudder to remember the class bully or hurtful words spoken by a classmate. Anything that makes a child or youth a target or makes them different from others can put them at high risk for feeling badly about themselves and their life.

To balance the "negative" experiences and "bad" feelings your child or youth may have when away from home, you will need to provide compliments, redirection, and a strong shoulder. Your child or youth needs a "safe" place to retreat. They need to know that they are loved as a person. They need to know that, while some of their behaviors are not acceptable, you love them for who they are and that love will not stop. Your home becomes their sanctuary.

Sometimes, when your child or youth has misbehaved or given you a hard time, it is difficult to find good things to say about them; things that would make them feel better about themselves. The great challenge is trying to build their self-esteem while not ignoring the inappropriate behaviors that are so often part of a mental health issue or disorder.

Helping Your Children and Youth Gain Self Confidence
- Encourage them to play sports, especially if they are athletic or have a good coach
- Enroll them in 4-H, church, or scouts where they can win awards for their work
- Send their good school papers to grandparents or others they love
- Look for 2 or 3 things a day to compliment them on
- Always talk positively about them in public and promote the GOOD attributes they possess
- Separate their disorder from their accomplishments
- Help them understand that everyone has differences and problems
- Encourage them to talk about how they feel about themselves and their friends

 **TRY THIS...**

- Help your child or youth on homework and school projects. Without doing the work for them, help by **providing guidance and making sure they do their best**. This will build their confidence and help minimize the chances of being made fun of by others.

- Help your child or youth **build or do a craft project**. Enter it in a fair or craft contest where everyone gets a ribbon.

- **Find a support group for children or youth** with emotional or mental health disorders. If there is not one in your area, ask a provider how one might be started.

- When you are at a loss and feel you need help, you can **ask a therapist or counselor for ideas** on building your child's or youth's self-esteem in a way that promotes unconditional love but does not condone bad behaviors.

- **Celebrate ALL accomplishments**. This will build your child's or youth's self-esteem and give positive reinforcement for behaviors that will help them now and in the future.

Growth and Development

"He was about 4 years old when I noticed he WAS different from other children. It was NOT in my mind and it was then that I started to learn everything I could about what was "normal" and what was different from other kids his age."

When a child or youth starts to show changes in their emotions and behavior, families often begin to wonder what behaviors are normal and which ones should be of concern. This is especially true with youth. Some families have to work hard to show that their child is normal while other families struggle to convince professionals, other family members, or friends that their child has a real problem and needs help. Deciding if your child's or youth's growth and development is in the normal range, or if he or she needs help can be challenging.

What is normal?

What is a concern?

There are significant differences among "typically developing" children and youth. These normal differences are due to a variety of factors, such as age, personality, culture, family tradition, beliefs, and the way children are raised. These factors can make it more difficult to decide if your child needs additional help in a specific developmental area. Whenever you are concerned about the growth and development of your child or youth, it is important to share these concerns with professionals that can help sort out what "is to be expected" or "normal" from what needs further attention. Often, families worry about a behavior only to learn that it is typical and that many other children do the same thing. But families may also be told that their child or youth has very troubling behaviors and should receive professional help. Let your "sense" be your guide and discuss anything you feel could be important to your child or youth's future. Your doctor, therapist, or school can give you information and guidance regarding age appropriate behaviors and developmental milestones.

WHAT YOU CAN DO TO HELP WITH YOUR 1 - 3 YEAR OLD'S DEVELOPMENT

- ❑ Find friends for playtime
- ❑ Leave your child with someone he or she knows for short periods
- ❑ Allow your child to keep their favorite toy with them as much as they want
- ❑ Leave a night light on in their bedroom
- ❑ Allow your child to be curious but safe
- ❑ Explain why things happen in simple terms
- ❑ Encourage your child to explain why he thinks things happen
- ❑ Gently correct your child's mistakes
- ❑ Include your child in simple chores like dusting, picking up clothes, etc.
- ❑ Praise your child often
- ❑ Show your child how much you love him or her
- ❑ Do not threaten your child
- ❑ Be consistent
- ❑ Set a regular bedtime (Children this age may sleep 10-15 hours with fewer naps)
- ❑ Read and play games with your child such as hide-and-seek or throwing a ball

WHAT YOU CAN DO TO HELP WITH YOUR 3 - 5 YEAR OLD'S DEVELOPMENT

- ❑ Enforce regular sleep hours to promote good sleeping habits
- ❑ Encourage your child to brush their teeth, bath, dress, and feed themselves
- ❑ Listen to your child's fears and feelings
- ❑ Give hugs and show affection
- ❑ Provide short and simple answers to questions
- ❑ Limit television and programs showing violence
- ❑ Focus on good behaviors
- ❑ Allow your child to help as much as possible
- ❑ Provide regular contact with other children (e.g., nursery school)
- ❑ Explain that television and movies are make-believe
- ❑ Set limits on behavior
- ❑ Offer choices
- ❑ Allow your child to express anger by voice (in words and in sounds)

❑ Discipline by taking away a favorite activity for a short period of time (like riding a bike)
❑ Help him or her prepare for school
❑ Play "make-believe" (play house, toy models, etc.)
❑ Read or do puzzles
❑ Color or do a craft together
❑ Go to the park or zoo, or take a walk

WHAT YOU CAN DO TO HELP WITH YOUR 5 - 11 YEAR OLD'S DEVELOPMENT

❑ Teach your child about eating the right kinds of food
❑ Encourage and arrange for your child to have activities outside of the home
❑ Require chores such as cooking or cleaning
❑ Set limits and impose consequences
❑ Provide information about sex when asked
❑ Allow your child to act in both mature and in immature ways
❑ Provide information about substance abuse and drugs
❑ Maintain family values and traditions
❑ Help your child explore and develop their talents like using the computer
❑ Praise and encourage your child often
❑ Limit TV, movies, and video games
❑ Encourage exercise and physical activity
❑ Enforce regular sleep hours to promote good sleeping habits
❑ Read to your child each night before bed

WHAT YOU CAN DO TO HELP WITH YOUR 11 - 15 YEAR OLD'S DEVELOPMENT

❑ Praise and encourage your child
❑ Talk with your child and allow them to bring up topics and issues to talk about
❑ Encourage your child to make his or her own decisions
❑ Be available for times when your child needs help or someone to talk to
❑ Compliment your child's achievements
❑ Listen to their interests, likes, dislikes without passing judgment (since these will probably change from day to day)
❑ Respect his or her privacy

❑ Allow independence while maintaining safety limits
❑ Provide concrete information about:
   -Sexuality
   -Body Changes
❑ Encourage games or other interests:
   -Intellectual Games
   -Reading
   -Arts, Crafts, Hobbies
   -Video Games (ones that are not violent)
   -Problem Solving Games
   -Computer
❑ Encourage regular exercise
❑ Maintain close contact with your child's school and teachers
❑ Know your child's friends
❑ Make your home a comfortable place for your child to bring friends

WHAT YOU CAN DO TO HELP WITH YOUR YOUTH OR YOUNG ADULT'S DEVELOPMENT
❑ Praise and encourage your young adult
❑ Talk with him or her, and allow the opportunity for your young adult to select what they would like to discuss
❑ Encourage your youth to make his/her own decisions
❑ Be available for when your youth needs you
❑ Compliment all achievements
❑ Listen to interests, likes/dislikes without passing judgment
❑ Respect his or her privacy
❑ Allow and encourage independence
❑ Provide information about:
   -Sexuality and body changes
❑ Encourage interests and support opportunities to explore them
❑ Encourage regular exercise
❑ Maintain close contact with school and teachers
❑ Know your youth's friends
❑ Make your home a comfortable place to bring friends
❑ Set chores and household rules WITH your young adult
❑ Share with your young adult how proud you are of his/her growth and independence
❑ Let him or her know you will always love them
❑ If arguments arise, listen to his or her side before responding

QUESTIONS YOU MAY ASK ABOUT YOUR CHILD OR YOUTH

- ❑ Does my child or youth act like others his or her age?
- ❑ Do other children like to spend time with my child or youth?
- ❑ Does my child or youth have a best friend or friends?
- ❑ Does my child or youth show emotions like other children the same age do?
- ❑ Does my child or youth seem to care about other people close to him or her?
- ❑ Has my child or youth had a complete check-up by a doctor to rule out illness?
- ❑ Do other children seem to be comfortable when they are around my child or youth?
- ❑ Is my child or youth extremely angry or anxious most of the time?
- ❑ Does my child or youth seem to have more fears than other children?
- ❑ Has my child's or youth's behavior suddenly changed in areas like school performance, eating or sleeping habits?
- ❑ Does my child or youth talk often about death and/or suicide?
- ❑ Does my child or youth have a need to do the same thing over and over again, like wash their hands?
- ❑ Does my child or youth seem to be exercising all the time, or constantly talking about the need to exercise?
- ❑ Does my child or youth often put him or herself in dangerous situations?
- ❑ Does my child or youth avoid family and friends and prefer to be alone most of the time?
- ❑ Does my child or youth talk about feeling and/or being worthless?
- ❑ Does my child or youth hear or see things that are not there?
- ❑ Does my child or youth think that "something" else is in control of his/her behaviors?
- ❑ Do I have reason to believe that my child or youth may have been sexually abused?

If answering these questions cause you to be concerned about your child or youth, it is important to get help as soon as possible. Call your doctor or school and ask for the name of someone with whom you can discuss these concerns and get assistance accessing necessary services and supports.

Developing Responsibility

"One day at clinic this kid younger than Shawn came out and made his own appointment. His mom stood there and nodded that the date and time would be OK, but he did it himself. It never occurred to me to encourage Shawn to start taking over some of his care."

As children grow up they are expected to take on new responsibilities. Your child or youth may not be ready right now to take on any new responsibilities, but he or she might surprise you. Children with special needs often require a period of time to adjust to changes in their responsibilities. Remember, children and youth who are given responsibilities tend to become independent much sooner than children and youth who have no experience taking care of themselves; Youth who have responsibilities have a good reason for feeling self-confident. Not all children and youth will be able to do the same things. It is important to give your child or youth the opportunity and support them in building their level of responsibility. Suggestions to help build responsibility:

Under the age of 5
- ❏ Simple chores, like letting the dog out or picking up towels
- ❏ Take care of toys and cleaning up at the table

Between 5-10 years
- ❏ Clean own room
- ❏ Help set the table
- ❏ Help clean up dishes
- ❏ Care for a pet
- ❏ Take messages to and from school

Between 10-15 years
- ❏ Learn about his/her special needs
- ❏ Take medication when asked
- ❏ Spend money or allowance
- ❏ Do more chores around home, like mow lawn or help fix meals
- ❏ Begin to participate in meetings, IEP's and other planning activities

Between 15-20 years
- ❑ Order own medication and make appointments
- ❑ Work for a few hours each day for pay
- ❑ Fix and clean up after meals; Do laundry
- ❑ Keep notes for doctor or therapist
- ❑ Serve as the lead for meetings regarding their future

It is important to teach your child or youth that a disorder is no excuse for not being responsible. Responsibility is an important step toward gaining independence. Without it, he or she will always need someone to care for them or, from your youth's perspective, will always have someone telling them what they can and what they cannot do.

 TRY THIS...

- Take your child or youth to the library or onto the Internet and **teach them to look up information on their disorder**. This information gives them a sense of power and control.

- Let your child or youth choose two jobs at home that they would like to do for the week. Youth are more likely to follow through if **they selected the chores**.

- Write down chores that are age appropriate on pieces of paper (each chore on a separate piece of paper) and drop these into a basket. Let your child or youth **"pull" two chores** (more if they are older) each morning. These will be their chores for that day. Some children and youth do better when they do not have to do the same thing day after day. The anticipation of not knowing what they will "pull" helps them look forward to being assigned a chore. They will also enjoy being in control of what chore they will do for that day.

- Teach your child and youth about **personal and social responsibility**. Take them to a gym or walk with them. Sign up for a "clean up day" and help them see how their responsible actions can help others. Work alongside them so they see that responsibility taking is important to you as well.

Notes

Moving On

"It seemed like we no more than got used to one program and she outgrew them and we were back to square one. We started to learn more about what was "normal" and how to move from one program to another without losing everything we had gained."

Your child or youth will probably "outgrow" the programs he or she is now in because of their age or other eligibility requirements. Your child may be transferred into other programs or services based upon their needs or what is available in your area. This is called transition. Your child or youth will transition many times during their life but an especially important transition occurs when he or she moves from the system that serves children/youth to the one that serves adults.

Transition Planning

"I wanted her to stay with her pediatrician...with all of the people that had always been on our team. But, she was growing up and wasn't eligible anymore. Even if she was, she wanted to pick her own doctors, her own programs."

Transition is not something that happens just <u>to</u> young adults...it is a process that involves the entire family. Preparing for the young adult years can be a new experience for many families. It can be a time to start talking about what will happen and who can help make sure your youth has the necessary services once they are no longer a child. Because every family is different, it is important that you take what you learn from this book and use it in a way that best meets your youth and family's goals.

What Transition Means
Transition means getting ready for a change. For you and your youth, that change means moving from the children's system of care to the adult system. These two systems are very different. You have already been through many transitions in your life. These include becoming a parent, starting your children in school, and helping your children as they move from elementary to middle schools.

Some professionals use the term "transition" to refer specifically to the move from school to work. Other professionals use the term "transition" to refer just to the move from pediatric to adult health care. But, in order for transitions to be successful, we need to make sure that all areas of the adult life are included in the transition process. This involves you, as a parent, playing an active role and:
- Gradually shifting responsibilities from you to your child/youth/young adult.
- Helping your youth make decisions that will impact their future.
- Developing a long-term plan starting at a young age to get ready for adult life.

Transition planning carefully looks at your youth's strengths, needs, and goals for the future. Using these as building blocks; the transition team will develop a plan that outlines where your youth is going, how they will get there, and what they will need along the way. This process cannot occur without the involvement of you or your youth.

Where Are They Going?
It probably seems like you have just learned about the system of care for children and now you having to get ready to move your youth into a new, unknown adult system. That system uses different doctors and providers, and works in a way that may be totally new to you. But, transition is a long-term process, not a single event – so you have time to learn and prepare.

Children begin transition before they ever leave the child system. Most often, children and their families should begin planning by age 14. You might think about the ages of 14-15 years as the "getting started" phase. The ages of 16-17 can be considered being "on their way". When they are age 18 and over they are the "almost there".

Transition involves changes in roles and responsibilities in all areas of living, including:

Financial Resources:
- Insurance
- Benefits/Income/Wages
- Draft Registration
- Supplemental Security Income (SSI)
- Guardianship
- Food Stamps
- Money Management
- Plan for Achieving Self Support (PASS)

Housing:
- Family Residence
- Independent Living
- Group Home
- Residential Care Facility

Recreation:
- Home
- Church
- Neighborhood
- Hobbies
- Clubs

Relationships:
- Co-Workers
- Advocates
- Family
- Professionals
- Friends

Independent Living:
- Transportation
- Domestic Activities
- Socialization and Sexuality

Health Care:
- Adult Primary Care
- Specialty Care
- Outpatient Services
- In Patient Services
- Medication
- Therapy and Counseling

Employment:
- Employment
- Supported Employment
- Volunteer Placement

Training & Education:
- College
- Adult Education
- Trade, Technical Schools
- Specific Vocational Training and Placement Programs
- Community Based Adult Day Programs

Professionals and agencies may be aware that your youth is moving from child to adult services but "the system" may not always put a process in place for making that move happen smoothly. Often the providers of child services are not the same ones as those for adults. Some youth find that when they turn 18 or 21 (depending on the state they live in) they are suddenly no longer eligible for the services they have been using. It is not unusual for youth to be declared ineligible for "children's services" before adult services are in place.

How Your Family Can Help

You are probably asking how you can help. You may be having trouble getting services and your youth may not be very helpful because of their mental health needs. Helping them, or getting them to allow you to help, may seem impossible. But, even if they do not see the importance, you must be the model. You can do this many ways, but always include them as the important part of the team. Your role as a parent is changing. Everything cannot and should not happen all at once!

Building Your Family's Role in Transition Planning
- ❏ Think about transition now.
- ❏ Build a personal circle of support.
- ❏ Explore beliefs about the future.
- ❏ Listen to what your teen is saying about the future.
- ❏ Find out what's available right now and what's possible for persons with mental health needs.
- ❏ Find resources.
- ❏ Talk with other families that have been or are going through transitions.
- ❏ Trust your instincts.
- ❏ Try new things. Be brave.
- ❏ Be organized in addressing transition. Make lists, plans, write down questions, and keep good records.

Getting Youth Involved in Their Transition

You can begin slowly in building your youth's readiness for transition. Make sure your youth:
- ❏ Understands their condition
- ❏ Knows the warning signs that mean they need emergency help
- ❏ Knows who to call when they need help

❏ Learns how to make their appointments
❏ Can order their medication
❏ Writes down questions for appointments and meetings
❏ Carries an insurance card and other important documents
❏ Understands their medications, side effects, and when to call the doctor
❏ Keeps a list of addresses and phone numbers of physicians, providers, and resources
❏ Understands why they need to shift to the adult system of care
❏ Participates as a full partner in the development of a transition plan
❏ Participates in meetings, such as at school, with providers, and others related to their transition
❏ Begins thinking about what they would like as an adult
❏ Learns about different educational programs after high school
❏ Starts talking to agencies that might help as they get older
❏ Begins thinking about work and what they want to do after school
❏ Begins doing activities in the home, school, and community that build on strengths and develop new skills
❏ Begins to develop work experience and job skills by working part time or volunteering
❏ Discusses how their condition might affect the kind of jobs they can do
❏ Is thinking about how to get around if they decide to move away from home

Overcoming Barriers

There will be problems and barriers that will get in the way of transition. It may be providers who cannot help you or problems getting the adult services set up before services from the children's system end. This is just a fact and a part of transition and change. Remember how hard it was when your child first began having problems? Think about all of the ways you had to work the system and the people that you needed to help you. This will be much the same. But, with team work and careful planning, barriers will be less of a problem and you will not have to face them alone.

It is common for families to serve as a "transition advocate" and make sure that their youth can fulfill their goals and dreams. To help make that happen, you must:

- Be aware that you will face barriers
- Be prepared to play a major role in resolving problems when they arise
- Be willing to commit time and energy to resolving problems
- Gather information about transition such as laws, regulations, policies, etc.
- Communicate clearly
- Trust your instincts
- Be persistent
- Stay involved and informed at every level
- Include your youth and serve as a role model and support
- Build a team of experts that can help make sure the right things happen
- Know what your options are when things do not go as planned

Looking at Services for Today and Tomorrow

Some of the services your youth gets in the child/youth mental health system may not be available when he or she is an adult. It is important to plan ahead, to help assure that your youth gets needed services when he or she is an adult. Use this chart to list what services your youth is currently receiving and who you will need to talk with as your youth transitions into adult programs.

Child and Youth Services We Get Now	Name of Person We Talk To about this Now	Adult Program That Could Provide This Service	Name of Contact at the Adult Program	Who Will Contact Them and When
FINANCIAL: List the programs or insurance that help pay for services				
MENTAL HEALTH SERVICES: List the mental health services your youth uses, like counseling, therapy, and others				
HEALTH CARE: List the health services your youth uses like a regular doctor and medication management				
TRAINING & EDUCATION: List where and how your youth is getting trained for a job or college				
OTHER: List other services or programs that help you meet your youth's needs				

SORTING IT OUT

It is important to look at all areas of adult life and make sure that you and your youth have the planning information you need. This chart helps you think about all of these areas and where you might get more information or help.

AREA	✅	WHAT WE NEED	WHO MIGHT HELP
Financial Resources: Resources to pay for expenses and needs			
Insurance			
Benefits/Income/Wages			
Supplemental Security Income (SSI)			
Guardianship			
Food Stamps			
Money Management			
Plan for Achieving Self Support (PASS) Ticket to Work			
Housing: A place to live as an adult			
Family Residence			
Independent Living			
Group Home			
Residential Care Facility			
Recreation: Support and resources for life as an adult			
Home			
Church			
Hobbies			
Clubs			
Relationships: Building skills and behaviors			
Co-Workers			
Advocates			
Family			
Professionals			
Friends			

Independent Living: Getting services and support to live as an adult			
Transportation			
Domestic Activities			
Socialization and Sexuality			
Health Care: Getting necessary adult health care services			
Adult Primary Care			
Specialty Care			
Outpatient Services			
In Patient Services			
Medication			
Therapy and Counseling			
Employment: Getting and keeping a job			
Employment			
Supported Employment			
Volunteer Placement			
Training & Education: Getting training and education			
College			
Adult Education			
Trade, Technical Schools			
Vocational Training and Placement Programs			
Community Based Adult Day Programs			
Other: Other things we feel we need help with			

Future Planning

"How long will she be ill? What if she needs help after we have died? Who would take care of her if I were not there? I can't imagine what her life would be like if she didn't have a family to watch out for her interests."

When a family includes a child or youth with special needs, parents need to consider and plan carefully for the future of that child, after they are gone. Your child or youth with mental health needs may continue to need help long after you are gone. You cannot assume that someone else will fill your role as a caretaker and advocate. Because death is usually not a planned event, it is never too early to start making plans for your children and youth in the event you are no longer around to care for them. The best way to start this kind of planning is to answer the following questions about how you would like things to be if you are not alive to take care of things.

Who will be my child's guardian?

By law, all children and youth under 18 and those who are unable to care for themselves must have a guardian. If you do not choose someone to be your child's guardian, the courts will do so if you die.

Where will my child or youth live?

When they ask themselves this question, many families realize that there are only a few options to choose from. If you do not have relatives or close friends who express an interest in taking your child or youth, then you will be faced with finding and recommending a suitable residential or group home placement. This decision should be documented ahead of time and updated as necessary to reflect your desire or your child or youth's needs.

Who will pay for the things my child or youth needs?

There are many things that residential programs do not cover for persons with special needs, such as over-the-counter medication, personal hygiene products, recreation, and others. These are the things that families traditionally pay for. Some families may have the means to set aside funds in a special account for future support in the event that they are gone. Others may have to depend upon public programs to help meet their child's or youth's needs. It is best to check ahead of time to see what help would be available and determine if that help would be adequate. Know the facts about programs that your child would be eligible for, in the event of your death; and plan ahead so there will be less for you to worry about.

Who will advocate for my child or youth?

While it is assumed that the guardian would advocate for your child or youth, you can also identify someone else to be an advocate. This can be especially helpful when your child or youth will be cared for in a residential or state-run institution or program, rather than a family home. Sometimes a Guardian Ad Litem can be appointed to look out for your child or youth's best interests.

How will I be sure that my wishes are followed?

The only way to ensure that your wishes are followed is through legal channels. A lawyer can draw up a will or help you with estate planning that would include provisions regarding care for your child or youth. If you have the money to do this, it will help ensure that your intentions are followed. If you do not have money to pay for legal services, ask Legal Aid to assist you. Legal Aid programs often provide this type of service at no cost or for a small fee and you can find them in your Yellow Pages or online. Also, one of your child's or youth's providers may be able to direct you to free or reduced legal help and estate planning services.

 **TRY THIS...**

- Watch for **free seminars** in the paper on Estate Planning or online. Sometimes these sessions focus on individuals with severe physical or intellectual disabilities, but the information can be used or adapted to plan for your child or youth as well.

- Request a "Futures Planning" night at the school and **invite professionals to talk about planning** and setting aside funds for your child or youth's future.

Difficult Times

"Some things hurt too much and are just too scary to talk about. I keep them hidden in a faraway place in my mind, hoping and praying that I never have to get them out and deal with them head on."

Life throws us a curve ball every now and then. You are dealing with one now: the mental or behavioral issues effecting your child or youth. Some things in life are difficult and we all hope that we won't have to deal with these things. But some of us have no choice. This section discusses some of life's most difficult challenges

Dealing with Conflicts

"I was so mad. They knew how I felt, but they went ahead and stopped his medication anyway. I had yelled, begged, and done everything humanly possible to make them see what it would do. Now that it is done, I hope they are willing to suffer the consequences. Too bad Demetrius has to suffer with them."

Disagreement and conflict are unavoidable. Everyone encounters conflicts with other person at one time or another. This happens whether you have a child or youth with emotional or mental health problems, or not. However, when piled on top of everything else your family is dealing with, even the smallest conflict can cause you great pain and suffering. This is especially true if the conflict involves child or youth and their services and treatments. Conflicts, when left unresolved, cause stress and anxiety, and can undermine the trust you have in the people who are supposed to be helping you.

Recognizing What Might Cause Conflict
When you know what causes conflict you can help prevent conflicts from occurring or from becoming a major problem.

- Conflicts can start small and seem harmless. You might have a nagging feeling that something is just not right.
- Some conflicts seem to explode out of nothing. One day there was no difficulty, and the next day you are hit with a problem.
- You may have a problem or conflict with someone, but the person you have an issue with may not have any idea that there is a problem. Or, it may be the other way around.
- Conflicts can begin with simple difference of opinion but can grow to the point that tensions affect everything, including the decisions that are made by the team or the professionals you work with.
- Conflicts can be as minor as a "difference of opinion" or as big as due process issues that may require the involvement of lawyers.

The key to minimizing and controlling conflict is to tackle it before it gets too big. Below are some ideas about how to do this.

Prevention

➢ Make sure you understand what others said and what they meant before you respond.

➢ Ask questions when you do not understand something.

➢ Never assume that others understand what you said; ask them if they understand and encourage them to ask questions.

➢ Be open to differences of opinion. Difference does not mean conflict.

Responding to Conflict

➢ Talk with the person/program staff with which you have a problem or disagreement.

➢ Most programs have a conflict resolution policy. Find out what the program is supposed to do to assist you in resolving the issues that lead to the conflict.

➢ Start where the problem began and talk to the person closest to the problem. Save talking with administrative staff for later, in case all else fails.

➢ Listen and be open, but also stand firm on anything you feel might hurt your child or youth.

➢ Develop a plan for dealing with the conflict.

➢ Write down and document all of your efforts to resolve the issue.

➢ When you feel you have done all you can do to resolve the issue on your own, start sharing your problem with other members of your team and with administrative staff, if necessary.

TRY THIS...

• Picture yourself sitting on a lifeguard stand (or balcony, tower, tree, or other place where you can see below), looking down upon the problematic situation. From here, you can **examine the issue and what everyone is doing** to solve the problem. Picture where you need to be, how you need to act, and who you need to work with. This exercise lets you "remove" yourself from the problem, and then reinsert yourself in the best position to bring about a positive resolution.

- Share your problem with someone who is neutral to the problem. Ask them to share different ways of looking at the situation and of reaching solutions. You might ask them to **assist in working with you** and the team to solve the problem.

- If it seems that you argue and disagree constantly with other team members, **turn the issue over to an advocate**. There are many state programs, organizations, and agencies that have trained advocates to assist families when they have conflicts involving a child with special needs

 # Conflict Response Tips

➲ **Conflict is not a way to get attention**
Find other ways to draw attention to issues and needs without using conflict as bait. Confrontation should be used only as a last resort, and then only when dealing with major issues and problems that can interfere with your child's or youth's treatment or recovery.

➲ **Threats are not effective**
This can get YOU into big trouble and allow the culprit a way out.

➲ **Do not take the law into your own hands**
Again, you will lose, and the real culprit will win.

➲ **Never do something that will embarrass your child or youth**
Children and youth embarrass easy. Make sure they understand what you feel needs to be done and encourage them to share ideas on how to resolve the issue without embarrassing them.

➲ **Start working on a solution at the point where the problem starts**
Begin where the problem occurs, not with the department head, boss, or president. Follow the chain of command (start at the bottom and move toward the top, one person at a time).

➲ **Pay attention to your child or youth**
Be careful to not brush off something your child or youth feels is important. They count on you to help them when they feel they cannot do something by themselves.

➲ **Always be completely truthful**
Never lie about something or twist the facts in order to win your fight. It will come back later to haunt you or make things worse in the long run.

➲ **Never put something in writing that you will regret later**
Once a letter or an email is sent, it belongs to the person you sent it to and can be made public.

➲ **Mean what you say and say what you mean**
Do not say something you may regret later. Be careful that you do not give people something they can use against you.

➲ **Finish what you start**
Resolving a conflict takes time and emotional energy. If you cannot finish...get help or decide it is not worth the fight.

 # PROBLEM SOLVING

Use this sheet to help you "process" conflict and develop a plan for reaching a solution. Have someone who is not part of the conflict listen to you explain your approach. They can offer insights that are based on the facts, rather than the issues that triggered the conflict in the first place

Date:	
Problem:	
Who it involves:	Their phone number:
What I can do about it:	
What I plan on doing (steps):	When:
1.	
2.	
3.	
Who will help:	Their phone number:
I will know the problem is resolved when or if:	

The Stigma of Mental Illness

"One lady told me that if I was a better parent, that Jenny would not have these problems. Even though I knew it was not my fault, I kept that thought in the back of mind for years."

Mental illness is still not well understood and some people blame parents for the mental health problems of their child. In the past, it was felt that if parents raised their children "right" they wouldn't experience any emotional disturbances. In spite of what mental health research has revealed, some people still have this. Many families are made to feel responsible for their child's problems. Other families blame themselves for what has happened to their child or youth. They feel that somehow they should have been able to stop it. This is called stigma. While we have come a long way and more people understand and accept mental illness for what it is, there is still a stigma attached to having a child or youth with mental, emotional, or behavioral problems.

Some cultures look at mental health disorders differently and there may be sigma or misunderstandings within a family due to family beliefs and traditions. It is important for you to understand your family's beliefs and traditions and what may have occurred in the past that might cause family members to stigmatize you and or your child or youth.

 **TRY THIS...**

- **Be prepared** with a response to those who do not understand mental illness or your child's or youth's condition.

- **Know about mental illness** including the causes, treatments, and prognosis (what will happen over time) so that you can respond to comments with accurate and up to date information.

- **Educate others** about mental health, especially those closest to you and your family. Make sure they have access to the correct information.

- Recommend resources to people who seem to misunderstand mental illness. **Give them an opportunity to learn** what they do not know.

- Accept the fact that some people do not want to understand mental illness. For whatever reason, they do not want to believe what science tells us about mental illness. **Do what you can** and then avoid them and their ignorance whenever possible.

Suicide

"I always felt that I should have known. I mean, he was one of my best friends and we spent three hours each day together at practice. After his suicide I would go over each and every thing he said that day to me. Then I would think about the past week and try to remember as long ago as I could. I never did remember anything he said that would have told us he was going to do it. But, I will always feel somewhat responsible for Jeremy's death. I should have known."

Suicide is one of the most feared aspects of emotional, behavioral, and mental disorders. But that fear is also experienced by parents whose children have no known mental illness. Unfortunately, suicide, like death, is seldom discussed. Your child or youth may have threatened or attempted suicide. The sad truth is that the suicide rate is much higher among those with a mental illness than it is for the general population.

The best way to deal with the reality that your child or youth may be at greater risk (and the fear that comes with this reality) is through education. Learn what might cause your child or youth to attempt suicide and the warning signs. These are your best defense. However, it is impossible for you to watch your child or youth 24 hours a day for the rest of his or her life. At some point, you will have to stand back with a watchful eye and trust that he or she will pay attention to the major signals that something is wrong and will take steps to get help.

Why Suicide?

A child or youth may attempt suicide because of:
- Disturbed thinking related to their mental illness
- Thoughts that make death appealing or seem like a reward.
- Psychosis and a belief that they are "super humans" who are above death
- Extreme unhappiness with their situation and a feeling it will never get any better
- Vulnerability to surroundings
- Feeling that life is hopeless

- Seeing death as an only option out of the pain they are experiencing
- A need to cry out for help (resulting in accidental death)

Some children and youth feel they can "stage" a suicide to draw attention to their situation and receive the help they feel they need. Unfortunately, many of these attempts go wrong (as was discovered with Jeremy in the above quote). Since they are often alone, there is no one around to intervene when things get out of hand.

Many children and youth with mental health issues behave in a risky manner. They often show little fear; drive too fast, drink too much, take potentially lethal amounts of drugs, play with guns, or climb to dangerous heights. It is as if they are daring "Death" to find them which, unfortunately, it sometimes does.

What may be seen by others as a minor problem, such as breaking up with a girlfriend, getting bad grades, or not making the team, could easily be a desperate situation for a child or youth with an emotional, behavioral, or mental disorder. They may internalize what happened and feel more worthless and hopeless.

Learning the signs of suicide is vital for all families today. It may not prevent every suicide, but it can help identify those children or youth who are more at risk and address their needs before they feel that they have to cry out for help.

Suicide Warning Signals
- Any threat of suicide
- Bragging about having no fear of death
- Persistent risky behaviors such as drinking and driving, playing with guns, climbing to high places
- Giving away favorite things
- Obsession with death in talk, activity, or personal poems or stories
- Making statements that start with "After I am gone..."
- Recent loss such as death, broken relationship, or friendship
- Expressing overwhelming feelings of guilt or shame
- Feelings that the world would be a better place without him/her
- Talk about losing control
- Serious changes in sleeping, eating, personality, or behavior

- Turning trivial things (a bad grade, what someone said, the way someone looked at him/her) into a big issue
- Signs of depression and hopelessness

NOTE: These are only a few warning signs. They could also suggest other problems besides a possible suicide attempt. If you suspect or fear your child or youth may be considering suicide, talk with a professional <u>immediately</u>. THIS IS AN EMERGENCY. It is better to be safe than sorry.

 TRY THIS...

- Suggest suicide as a **topic for adult discussion** at a support group meeting, group therapy, or other gathering. Request that a professional come and discuss and answer questions. Bringing suicide out in the open is a good step toward prevention.

- Talk honestly with your child's or youth's service providers about your fears. They can help **watch for warning signs** and guide you on what to do should you have a reason to be alarmed.

- **Never take your child's or youth's problems or comments lightly.** Things that are extremely important to them might seem trivial to us. Young people may not have the ability to see the differences between big problems and little ones. When there is a lot going on in their lives, one more little thing may be enough to push them "over the edge". When your child or youth struggles with a problem, ask them to talk with you or someone else they trust about how to deal with it.

Notes

Behavioral, Emotional and Mental Disorders: The Name Game

"At first I begged for a diagnosis, a label, anything to blame what was happening. Now I wish we never even heard of schizophrenia."

There are many types of behavioral, emotional, and mental health disorders and conditions that can affect children and youth. Each year, new causes are discovered and different treatments are approved. This section provides an introduction to the major mental health disorders and includes fact sheets that you can copy and give to others, to help them understand on your child's or youth's disorder. This section was developed using material developed by the U.S. Substance Abuse and Mental Health Services Administration (SAMHSA).

Mental Illness and Emotional Disturbance

A child or youth with mental health needs can be defined as one who has a serious emotional disturbance (SED), an emotional disturbance, or behavioral disorder, or who is at risk of an emotional, behavioral, or mental health disorder. Since laboratory tests, and brain scans are not effective in diagnosing mental illness or behavioral/emotional problems, these disorders are often more difficult to identify than other medical disorders. The diagnosis of mental, emotional, and behavioral disorders in children or youth is typically based on information from parents, provider reports, results from a "mental status" examination, and clinician observation. These all provide clues that are considered by a clinician (e.g. psychiatrist or clinical psychologist) in making a diagnosis.

Mental health conditions are often referred to as a disorder, rather than as a disease, because diagnosis is based on observation and "functional impairments" rather than results from a set laboratory tests. A "Functional Impairment" (FI) is a problem or limitation that cannot be adequately explained by intellectual, sensory, or other health factors. Functional Impairments include the inability to create or maintain relationships with peers and teachers; engaging in improper behavior; having feelings that are inappropriate for the circumstances; a pervasive mood of unhappiness or depression; and, the development of physical symptoms or fears associated with personal or school problems. The definition of "mental illness" that is used by federal and state agencies and local programs is often tied to funding criteria, such as that used by Medicaid or Special Education.

Causes of Emotional & Mental Health Problems

Years ago, many professionals believed that mental health problems in adults or children and youth were caused by parents who had done a poor job of raising their children. Parents were blamed for giving in to the child or youth too much or spoiling them. But there were also those that were accused of punishing too harshly. Some were told they were overprotective and didn't give their children enough room to grow. At the same time, other families faced accusers who told them they didn't pay enough attention. As women entered the work force, many of them were blamed for their children or youth's problems. The ability to raise a healthy child or youth became associated with being a good parent. Unfortunately, while great strides have been made to educate and change this attitude, too many families are still made to feel that they are the primary cause of their child's or youth's problems, either by other family members, professionals working with them, or by themselves. The answer to the causes of mental and emotional disorders that children and youth face is not that simple.

Based on years of research, we know now that there is no single cause of most mental and emotional problems in children and youth. However, we do know that that the more negative factors a child or youth has to deal with, the higher the possibility of experiencing emotional or mental health problems. Research also shows that positive factors, such as a supportive family and appropriate services, can greatly reduce the negative impact that an emotional or mental health disorder has on a child or youth.

A brief explanation of three factors often associated with child or youth mental health disorders are discussed below.

Biological/Organic
Some emotional and mental health disorders appear to be closely associated with nutrition, medical problems, or an injury or illness shortly after birth. Some mental and emotional disorders in children or youth are the result of actual organic or chemical abnormalities within the brain. Organic causes can include brain malformations, chemical imbalances within the brain, or chemical imbalances that affect the functioning of the brain. Some children and youth with developmental disabilities have a behavioral or emotional disorder as well.

Hereditary
The tendency for a person to develop some mental health disorders can be inherited. Sometimes a gene is passed from the parent to the child that may cause the development of mental health disorders. Not every child or youth receiving the gene or who has a parent with a mental illness develops the disorder, but research shows the chances of having a mental health disorder is greater than that of the general population.

Environmental

Mental health and emotional problems in children and youth can be caused by the environment around them. Sometimes these are referred to as social factors. Environmental or social factors include being exposed to ongoing violence in the home or neighborhood, relationships with peers, economics, problems in school, and problems within the family.

Disorder Factsheets

The ten fact sheets on pages 103-113 briefly describe different types of mental health disorders in children and youth. These fact sheet should not be used to diagnose a mental health disorder, and do not include the full range of symptoms and treatments. Keep in mind that new research can yield rapid changes in our understanding of and approaches to mental disorders. You need to work closely with your child's or youth's providers on diagnosis, treatment and emerging issues.

There are many other mental health conditions in addition to those discussed on the ten fact sheets. You can learn more about these and other disorders from the internet or at your local library. You can also ask your child's or youth's providers for more information on specific conditions and disorders.

Attention-Deficit/Hyperactive Disorder

Children and youth with attention-deficit/hyperactivity disorder have difficulty controlling their behavior in school and social settings. These conditions can affect their ability to concentrate, learn, and maintain a normal level of activity. A diagnosis of attention-deficit, hyperactivity, or attention-deficit/hyperactivity disorder is usually made when children have several symptoms that begin before age 7 and last at least 6 months. The most common type is combined attention-deficit/hyperactivity disorder, which, as the name implies, is a combination of the inattentive and the hyperactive-impulsive types.

Signs and Symptoms may include:
Children and youth with the inattentive type disorder may:
- ✓ Have a short attention spans
- ✓ Be distracted easily
- ✓ Not pay attention to details
- ✓ Fail to finish things
- ✓ Have trouble remembering things
- ✓ Not seem to listen
- ✓ Not be able to stay organized

Children and youth with the hyperactive-impulsive type disorder may:
- ✓ Fidget and squirm
- ✓ Be unable to stay seated or play quietly
- ✓ Run or climb too much or at inappropriate times
- ✓ Talk too much or when they should not
- ✓ Blurt out answers before questions are completed
- ✓ Have trouble taking turns
- ✓ Interrupt others

Treatment
- ▪ Applied behavior analysis services
- ▪ Counseling/psychotherapy
- ▪ Special education programs
- ▪ Medication
- ▪ Combination of the above

Anxiety Disorder

Many children and youth experience anxiety at some point in their lives and some nervousness in anticipation of a situation such as the first day of school or a big test. However, when a child or youth cannot stop constant worries, or if the feelings interfere with everyday activities, they may have an anxiety disorder. When a child or youth spends at least six months worried excessively about everyday problems a professional may diagnoses them with an anxiety disorder. Anxiety is among the most common, most treatable mental disorders.

Signs and Symptoms may include:
- ✓ Chronic, exaggerated worry, tension, and irritability that appear to have no cause
- ✓ More intense worry than the situation warrants
- ✓ Physical signs, such as
    - Restlessness
    - Trouble falling or staying asleep
    - Headaches
    - Trembling
    - Twitching
    - Muscle tension
    - Sweating

Treatment
- Cognitive behavioral therapy
- Relaxation techniques
- Biofeedback to control muscle tension
- Counseling/psychotherapy
- Medication
- Combination of the above

Bipolar Disorder

Bipolar Disorder, also known as manic-depressive illness, is a serious disorder that causes shifts in a child's or youth's mood, energy, and ability to function. Different from the normal ups and downs that everyone goes through, the symptoms of bipolar disorder are severe. Bipolar disorder is marked by an ongoing combination of extremely high (manic) and low (depressive) moods. The highs may alternate with the lows, or both extremes may exist at the same time. Signs and Symptoms may include:

Manic symptoms:
- ✓ Severe changes in mood-unusually happy or silly; or very irritable, angry, agitated or aggressive
- ✓ Unrealistic highs in self-esteem – such as feeling or acting all powerful, like a superhero with special powers
- ✓ Increase in energy and the ability to go with little or no sleep for days without feeling tired
- ✓ Increase in talking - talking too much, too fast, changing topics too quickly, and cannot be interrupted
- ✓ Attention moves constantly from one thing to the next
- ✓ Repeated high risk-taking behavior; such as, abusing alcohol and drugs, reckless driving, or sexual promiscuity

Depressive symptoms:
- ✓ Irritability, depressed mood, persistent sadness, frequent crying
- ✓ Thoughts of death or suicide
- ✓ Loss of enjoyment in favorite activities
- ✓ Frequent complaints of physical illnesses such as headaches or stomach aches
- ✓ Low energy level, fatigue, poor concentration, complaints of boredom
- ✓ Major change in eating or sleeping patterns

Treatment
- ▪ Applied behavior analysis services
- ▪ Psychotherapy
- ▪ Medication
- ▪ Possible inpatient care
- ▪ Combinations of the above

Conduct Disorder

Children and youth who act out their feelings or impulses toward others in destructive ways may be diagnosed as having a conduct disorder. Children and youth with this disorder have great difficulty following rules and behaving in a socially acceptable way. **Their offenses tend to get more serious over time.** They are often viewed by other children, youth, adults and social agencies as "bad" or delinquent, rather than having a mental health disorder.

Signs and Symptoms may include:
- ✓ Steals and breaks the law
- ✓ Consistently lies
- ✓ Deliberately sets fires
- ✓ Often skips school
- ✓ Deliberately destroys other's property
- ✓ Uses weapons
- ✓ Battles with authority
- ✓ Won't follow rules
- ✓ Often aggressive
- ✓ May display inappropriate sexual behavior
- ✓ May behave in an anti-social manner

Treatment
- ▪ Applied behavior analysis services
- ▪ Special education programs
- ▪ Specific social skill and behavior programs
- ▪ Psychotherapy, including behavior and play therapy
- ▪ Family therapy
- ▪ Medication
- ▪ Combinations of the above

Depression

Children and youth can have depression. Depression is defined as a disorder when the feelings of depression persist and interfere with a child's or youth's ability to function. Children and youth under stress, who experience loss, or who have attention, learning, conduct or anxiety disorders are at a higher risk for depression. Depression also tends to run in families. The behavior of depressed children and youth may be different from that of depressed adults.

Signs and Symptoms may include:
- ✓ Frequent sadness, tearfulness, crying
- ✓ Decreased interest in activities; or inability to enjoy favorite activities
- ✓ Hopelessness
- ✓ Persistent boredom; low energy
- ✓ Social isolation, poor communication
- ✓ Low self-esteem and guilt
- ✓ Extreme sensitivity to rejection or failure
- ✓ Increased irritability, anger, or hostility
- ✓ Difficulty with relationships
- ✓ Frequent complaints of physical illnesses such as headaches and stomachaches
- ✓ Frequent absences from school or poor performance in school
- ✓ Poor concentration
- ✓ Major changes in eating and/or sleeping patterns
- ✓ Talk of or efforts to run away from home
- ✓ Thoughts or expressions of suicide or self-destructive behavior

Treatment
- ▪ Counseling/psychotherapy, including cognitive therapy
- ▪ Medication
- ▪ Applied behavior analysis services
- ▪ Possible inpatient care

Eating Disorders

The two most common eating disorders are anorexia nervosa (an obsession to be thinner) and bulimia nervosa (forcing oneself to throw up after binge eating). Bulimia nervosa can also include the abusive use of diuretics, laxatives, rules about eating, or extreme exercising. These disorders are characterized by a preoccupation with food and a distortion of body image. The incidence of anorexia and bulimia nervosa has increased significantly among teen and adult women over the last two decades, but can affect boys as well.

Signs and Symptoms may include:
- ✓ Intense fear of being overweight
- ✓ Feeling overweight, even when of normal or below normal weight
- ✓ Extremely low weight
- ✓ Loss of menstruation
- ✓ Excessive exercising
- ✓ Constipation
- ✓ Hair loss
- ✓ Lowered heart rate and body temperature
- ✓ Excessive use of laxatives and diet pills
- ✓ Gorging and then vomiting

Treatment
- ▪ Applied behavior analysis services
- ▪ Counseling/psychotherapy
- ▪ Medication
- ▪ Medical care through a primary care physician
- ▪ Possible inpatient care
- ▪ Self-help groups
- ▪ Working with a nutritionist
- ▪ Family therapy
- ▪ Combinations of the above

Obsessive Compulsive Disorder

Obsessive-compulsive disorders (OCD) involve repeated patterns of thoughts or processes resulting in repetitive behaviors or rituals. More than 2.5% of the population is felt to have some form of OCD. This disorder typically begins in the teen or early adult years, but occurs more frequently in younger children than previously thought. This disorder can be chronic (ongoing), or acute (start suddenly, disappear for a period, then reappear).

Signs and Symptoms may include:
- ✓ Over-concern that harmful events, such as death or disease, might occur
- ✓ Checking and washing rituals
- ✓ Counting items over and over
- ✓ Putting on and taking off clothing repeatedly
- ✓ Preoccupation with rituals to the extent that it seriously interferes with the ability to participate in daily activities

Treatment
- ▪ Applied behavior analysis services
- ▪ Psychotherapy
- ▪ Medication
- ▪ Combinations of the above

Schizophrenia

Schizophrenia is a serious psychiatric illness with symptoms that include strange and disorganized thinking, strange feelings, and unusual behavior. It is not common in children and is difficult to recognize in its early stages. The behavior of children or youth with schizophrenia may differ from that of adults and can change slowly over time, making diagnosis and treatment difficult.

Signs and Symptoms may include:
- ✓ Trouble telling dreams from reality
- ✓ Seeing and hearing things that are not real
- ✓ Vivid and bizarre thoughts and ideas
- ✓ Extreme moodiness
- ✓ Believes others are "out to get them"
- ✓ Confusing television with reality
- ✓ Severe anxiety and fearfulness

Treatment
- Psychotherapy
- Medication
- Possible inpatient care
- Combinations of the above

Separation Anxiety Disorder

Separation anxiety is when a child or youth exhibits an intense anxiety to the point of panic, as the result of being separated from a parent or a loved one. It can suddenly appear in a child or youth who has shown no previous signs of a problem, be the result of some traumatic event, or due to any number of factors that the child or youth cannot explain. This anxiety is so intense that it interferes with the child's or youth's normal activities.

Signs and Symptoms may include:
- ✓ Refuses to leave the house alone
- ✓ Clings to parents or loved one and "shadows" them
- ✓ Fears that someone they love may die
- ✓ Complains of illness or other problem as an excuse to stay close
- ✓ May have heart palpitations or other physical signs of distress
- ✓ Has trouble falling asleep
- ✓ Have fears of harm or death

Treatment
- ▪ Applied behavior analysis services
- ▪ Psychotherapy including play therapy
- ▪ Medication
- ▪ Combinations of the above

Tourette's Syndrome

Tourette Syndrome is defined by having various motor and vocal tics (involuntary movements) that last for more than one year. The most common first symptom is a facial tic (eye blink, nose twitch, grimace), and is replaced or added to by other tics of the neck, trunk, and limbs. These movements are out of the child or youth's control and may also involve the entire body, as in kicking and stamping. Other symptoms such as touching, repetitive thoughts and movements and compulsions can occur. There may also be verbal tics (noises, words, or sounds) that usually occur with the movements. These may include grunting, throat clearing, shouting and barking.

Signs and Symptoms may include:
- ✓ Facial tics, such as rapidly blinking eyes
- ✓ Involuntary sounds, like clearing the throat or sniffing
- ✓ The use of inappropriate or unacceptable words
- ✓ Jumping
- ✓ Stamping
- ✓ Making obscene gestures
- ✓ Mimicking the gestures of other persons
- ✓ Repetition of a word or phrase
- ✓ Repeating other people's words

Treatment
- ▪ Applied behavior analysis services
- ▪ Psychotherapy
- ▪ Medication
- ▪ Combinations of the above

QUESTIONS YOU MAY WANT TO ASK ABOUT YOUR CHILD'S OR YOUTH'S DIAGNOSIS

You probably have many questions related to your child or youth's diagnosis. You may be so overwhelmed that you forget to ask questions when you go to appointments. Remember that questions can be asked anytime. Below are some questions that you can use to get the information you need to help you understand your child's or youth's diagnosis or disorder better. Some families ask the same questions over and over again, to make sure that they really understand the information that they are being given.

- ❏ What makes you think my child or youth has this condition?
- ❏ What evaluations, assessments, or tests support this diagnosis?
- ❏ Could it be anything else?
- ❏ What caused it?
- ❏ Did we do anything wrong?
- ❏ How long will he or she have it?
- ❏ Will my child or youth ever be like other kids?
- ❏ What kinds of treatments work the best?
- ❏ Will my child or youth get worse before getting better?
- ❏ What if my child or youth doesn't respond to treatment?
- ❏ Can you give me some information on this disorder?
- ❏ Can we talk with another family with a child or youth with this disorder?
- ❏ What do we tell the school, family, and friends?
- ❏ Will our other children have it too?
- ❏ Will you continue to work with us or will you refer us to someone new?
- ❏ Can we call you later if we have more questions?

Notes

Your Child's or Youth's Education

> "I quit going to parent teacher conferences years ago. I just could not stand another meeting feeling like I had somehow let down my child and the school. I didn't know what I was supposed to do about helping him learn. All I knew was that he wasn't and it was my fault."

School is one thing that most children, youth, and families have in common. Children and youth have a legal right to receive an education. Sometimes educational services are provided in a public school. Your home may be your child's or youth's school or they might attend a specialized school. No matter where your child or youth attends school the law provides certain protections and supports to make sure the educational services they receive are "free and appropriate". This section talks about these protections and how your child's or youth's education can be individualized to meet their unique needs.

Special Education

"School was a nightmare until we had a meeting and developed a plan that spelled out exactly what Rob would get, how he would get it, and who would be helping him each step of the way. It made all of the difference for him and for us."

Like any other disorder, mental health problems can cause a disruption in the education of your child or youth. Since children spend a majority of their waking hours in school, this disruption can have severe consequences. However, school can also be a place of treatment, a form of respite, and still meet the goal of educating your child or youth.

Schools are required by state and federal laws to serve students with special educational needs for free and in an appropriate manner. This is called a free and appropriate public education (FAPE). It means that the school must take certain measures to ensure that your child or youth is getting the same opportunities as other children without a disability to get an education. This is part a federal law called the "Individuals with Disabilities Education Act" or IDEA. This law outlines what the school must do to identify and serve children and youth with special needs. States receive money from the federal government to help pay for the costs of educating children with special needs appropriately. If a state does not comply with the requirements of this law, the state could lose these funds. State education laws explain how children and youth should be identified and educated in your local public school.

Evaluation for Eligibility
In order for a student to be eligible for special education services, the student must receive a full evaluation by a team to determine if they have an emotional, behavioral, or mental health disorder that is covered by the state education plan and that will/is now adversely affecting their ability to learn in a regular education classroom.

The Evaluation Process
- You or a member of the school staff may make the request for an evaluation.

- The school will send you paperwork to get your permission to evaluate your child or youth. You must give consent in writing for the first evaluation.
- The evaluation includes information that you provide to the team, assessments (tests), medical concerns, and interviews with you and school staff who know your child or youth.

The evaluation must:

- Be completed by trained and knowledgeable persons;
- Include all areas related to a suspected area of disability;
- Include more than just one test or assessment procedure;
- Use the child's native language unless it is clearly not possible to do so; and
- Not discriminate because of the child's or youth's race or culture.

Determining Eligibility

When the evaluation is finished, school staff are supposed to talk with you about the results. The results from the evaluation will help you and school staff to decide if your child needs special education services and will show what kind of services may help. If you do not agree with the results or the school's decision regarding what services your child or youth needs you can ask that another evaluation be done by someone who does not work for the school. This is called an Independent Educational Evaluation (IEE).

Not all students who receive an evaluation will be determined to be eligible for special education services. This may be due to the evaluation results, the diagnosis, or an agreement between you and the school. Even if your child or youth is determined to be eligible, you may decide that your child's or youth's educational needs can be met without special education services. In this case, you will need to work closely with the school to develop a strategy on meeting your child or youth's needs within the regular education arena. A meeting with teachers and the school principal or counselor to discuss how your child or youth's disorder may impact their school performance is a great way to start. Many families and schools have developed creative plans for assisting students to be successful and learn despite their emotional problems.

Developing a Plan

All students receiving special education services must have an Individualized Education Program (IEP). The IEP is the plan that will outline what services your child or youth will need in school to meet their educational goals. To do this the school must set up a meeting to discuss the results of the evaluation with you and develop a plan on how special services should be used to assist your child or youth learn.

A number of people should be invited to the IEP meeting. This group is called the IEP team. The school district will let you know who they expect to attend. The following people are typically included as members of the IEP team:

- You and other significant members of your family
- Your child or youth
- Your child's or youth's regular education teacher
- Your child's or youth's special education teacher or special education provider
- A person from the school district who is qualified to provide or supervise special education
- Someone who understands what the evaluation means and can talk about the what your child or youth may need
- Others that you or the school invites because they know your child or youth and can assist in planning for their educational needs.
- Anyone of your choice, such as a friend, an advocate, or service provider. (You have the right to include anyone of your choosing on your child's or youth's IEP team)

The IEP cannot be written before the team meets and it needs to include the following:

- A statement of your child's or youth's current level of educational performance
- Annual educational goals
- Short term objectives (or activities) to help your child or youth reach the goals
- A description of the services to be provided
- Information on where these services will be provided
- An explanation concerning how, when, and where your child or youth will participate in regular education programs
- The date that the services will begin
- The way it will be determined if each of the goals has been accomplished

The plan must identify and describe any and all services that the school will provide in their efforts to educate your child or youth. The IEP must be re-evaluated at least once a year, but can be re-evaluated sooner if the educational needs of your child or youth require a change in the setting where services are provided or in the plan's goals. If the services are changed this must be documented in the IEP plan.

Re-evaluations and Annual IEP Meetings and Plans

If a your child or youth is receiving special education services through an IEP, they must be re-evaluated to determine if there is still a need for special education, and to address any new needs that arise. This should not occur more than once a year, unless you and the school district agree that one is needed, but should happen at least once every three years, unless you and the school district agree that it is not needed.

You will meet with the IEP team at least once per year to discuss progress and include all new goals or services into the IEP plan for your child or youth.

Due Process

If you believe that your child's or youth's rights are being violated because they are not receiving the services they need or the services they receive are inappropriate, you can follow a procedure called "due process". This process was established to assist families in assuring that their child or youth is receiving appropriate and individualized services based upon their needs. Your child's or youth's school must provide you with information on how to activate due process.

Functional Behavior Assessments and Interventions

Children and youth with emotional, behavioral, and mental health disorders often struggle to manage their behaviors in school. Psychologists and educators have developed a process to learn about how children and youth develop problem behaviors is called "Functional Behavioral Assessment" (FBA). Learning about the behaviors and knowing when and where they are likely to happen allows professionals to plan strategies to teach children and youth new, positive behaviors. These strategies are called positive behavioral interventions. Schools use the FBA to evaluate and address behavioral issues that can interfere with education and learning.

The 2004 Individuals with Disabilities Education Act (IDEA) states that the IEP Team must consider the use of FBA and positive behavioral interventions and supports, and other strategies, in cases where a student's behavior impedes their learning or that of others. A positive behavioral intervention is implemented before a problem behavior occurs, thus precluding the need for punishment. Examples of positive behavioral interventions include changing where a student sits in the classroom, adjusting the amount or content of schoolwork or homework, or rewarding the student for positive behaviors. The goal of this approach is to stop or reduce the frequency of problem behaviors so that punishment is not necessary.

Functional behavioral assessment (FBA) is a process for collecting information that will assist in developing an intervention. The data collected on your child or youth in a FBA is used to help determine why problem behaviors occur and help identify ways to address the behaviors. IDEA specifically requires an FBA be carried out whenever a student has their current placement changed for disciplinary reasons. The evaluation requirements of IDEA make it clear that children and youth must be evaluated in all areas related to a suspected disability. This means that if your child or youth has problem behaviors that are not improving, they may need an evaluation to examine the behaviors more closely. You may request an FBA if your child's or youth's problem behaviors are becoming worse, when the team cannot explain to you why the problem behaviors occur, or when the behaviors are interfering with their ability to learn.

The professionals who complete a functional behavioral assessment may use different ways to collect information. School staff may interview you and your child or youth. They observe your child or youth in different settings, such as the lunchroom or classroom, or on the playground and gather reports from teachers and others. The team reviews your child's records, including any information you would like to share with them.

The results of this process should lead to ideas about why the problem behaviors occur. Assessment results should then be used to develop a positive behavior intervention plan.

Functional Behavioral Assessment Steps

The Individuals with Disabilities Education Act (IDEA) does not describe exactly how a functional behavioral assessment is to be done. The process will vary somewhat based on the needs of the student. However, the following overview identifies steps that are generally agreed to be necessary parts of this kind of assessment.

The process begins with an **identification of the specific behaviors** that must change. If a child or youth has many problem behaviors you and other team members should focus on the one or two most serious behaviors (the ones that interfere most with learning).

The **problem behaviors are described** in a way that helps everyone on the team to understand the behavior(s) and the overall impact these behaviors have on your child or youth and the specific impact they have on his or her learning. Typically these steps involve:
- Identifying and agreeing on the behavior(s) most in need of change.
- Determining when and where these behaviors occur.
- Clarifying when and where these behaviors do NOT occur.
- Identifying what may contribute to your child's or youth's behaviors.
- The team will ask questions like:
  - What is unique about where behaviors do and do not occur?
  - Could they be related to how your child or youth get along with others in that setting?

- · Does the number of other students in the setting contribute to the problem?
  - · Is the amount of work your child or youth is asked to do cause the problem?
  - · Could the time of day affect the behaviors?
  - · Was there a problem or a disagreement that caused or contributed to the behavior?
  - · Are the behaviors likely to occur in a specific set of circumstances or a specific setting?
  - · What events seem to cause the problem behaviors?
- Collecting information from as many sources as possible.
- Developing an idea about why the problem behaviors occur (the function of the behaviors).
- Testing this idea by using positive behavioral interventions that are written into your child's or youth's IEP or behavior intervention plan.
- Evaluate the success of the interventions to reduce these target behaviors.
- Change or adjust the interventions as needed.

Behavior Intervention Plan

A behavior intervention plan (this may be called a behavior support plan or positive intervention plan) is used to teach or reinforce positive behaviors. Typically, a child's or youth's team develops the plan. It usually includes:

- How to develop skills to increase proper behavior
- Changes to be made in classrooms or other school settings to reduce or end problem behaviors
- Approaches to replace problem behaviors with appropriate behaviors
- Supports to help your child or youth use the appropriate behaviors

Behavioral Crises

If your child or youth has behaviors that place them or others in danger, a crisis intervention plan should be developed. Remember, plans must be developed before they are needed. The team should decide what behaviors constitute a crisis and what should be done. By having a plan in place that guides actions, teachers can help your child or youth through difficult emotional situations if they should arise.

School Discipline Policies

A positive behavior intervention plan is not a plan to determine what happens to your child or youth when they violate a rule or code of conduct. That would be called a discipline plan or a punishment plan. The IEP team should examine the school discipline policies and discuss what school policies need to be amended with respect to your child or youth, based upon their individual needs. The team may decide that the penalties need to be different from those written into the school policy. This decision to amend school policy must be based on your child's or youth's evaluation and a complete review of his/her school records.

Sometimes general school discipline policies will not be successful in correcting your child's or youth's problem behaviors. If school staff wants to use a "standard" discipline procedure, you should ask for information and evidence that support the use of that "standard" procedure.

Zero-Tolerance Policies

Some school districts have zero-tolerance policies that provide immediate consequences for specific behaviors. Consequences for problem behaviors must not discriminate against your child or youth based on his or her disability. The IEP team is responsible for deciding if an exception needs to be made to the written school district discipline policy for your child or youth and if he/she should have a consequence for misbehaviors that is different from the one written into the school discipline policies. Further, instructional goals may need to be written into the IEP as part of the overall effort to remediate the problems your child or youth is having following school policies on student behavior.

Some administrators may not want to make exceptions to school discipline policies that have been established for all students. But, with your child or youth, exceptions may be necessary. Your child or youth may need to have individualized consequences that are more effective in supporting positive behaviors. You should examine school policies to help determine if modifications need to be made to meet the needs of your child or youth.

Tips to Assist You in the Special Education Process

If you feel that your child or youth has a problem that may interfere with learning:
- ❑ Call the school and set up an appointment with the teacher
- ❑ Request that the school evaluate your child or youth for special education services

During the time your child or youth is being evaluated:
- ❑ Fill out all papers and sign releases
- ❑ Ask how the information will be used
- ❑ Ask questions and get answers about anything you do not understand
- ❑ Provide information that may help them understand your child's or youth's needs

After the evaluation:
- ❑ Request a copy of all evaluation results
- ❑ Ask someone to explain the results to you (and your youth)
- ❑ Let the school know when and where you would like to have the IEP planning meeting
- ❑ Ask the school who will be attending the IEP planning meeting
- ❑ Let the school know the name and role of everyone you are going to invite to the IEP planning meeting

At the IEP Planning Meeting:
- ❑ Bring all information you feel will help the team
- ❑ Come prepared to participate as a full team member
- ❑ Request that your youth attend so she/he can be a member of the planning team
- ❑ Make sure you know who everyone is and their role
- ❑ Make sure that the IEP Plan was not filled out prior to the meeting
- ❑ Ask questions about anything you do not understand
- ❑ Review and consider the recommendations
- ❑ Ask to see the proposed classroom and to meet the teacher
- ❑ Ask when and where your child or youth will be with students that are not in a special program
- ❑ Ask how the goals will help your child or youth learn
- ❑ Ask if your child or youth will receive a regular diploma
- ❑ Ask if your child will receive accommodations for state mandated testing.
- ❑ Ask what discipline will be used with your child
- ❑ Request to speak to another parent whose child or youth is in the program

❑ Make sure you understand and agree to what is written in the document before you sign it

❑ State that you need to have a day or two to review and think before signing

❑ Make sure everything you feel your child or youth needs has been brought up and discussed

After the IEP Meeting:

❑ Meet with the teacher to set up a way of sharing information and updates

❑ Help your child or youth understand their special needs

❑ Share changes or needs with the school as they arise

❑ Visit the classroom or volunteer at the school

❑ Review the goals on the IEP plan with the teacher periodically (once every two months)

❑ Request another IEP meeting if progress is not occurring as expected

PARENTAL RIGHTS IN SPECIAL EDUCATION

As the parent of a child or youth receiving exceptional student education you have the right to:

- ✓ Participate in the development of the IEP Plan and the annual review
- ✓ Help set the time and place of the meeting
- ✓ Have meetings conducted in the language you choose
- ✓ Receive accommodations for any disability you may have (i.e. a hearing impairment, visual impairment, need to use a wheelchair)
- ✓ Give your consent before any evaluations are performed
- ✓ Receive a copy and explanation of all evaluations
- ✓ Seek an independent evaluation at public expense if the school's evaluation seems inappropriate
- ✓ Require written consent for planned activities for your child or youth
- ✓ Receive written notice of proposed changes in the placement of your child or youth
- ✓ Attend and comment at all hearings that are held concerning the state's plan for education
- ✓ Review and request a copy of all of your child's or youth's records
  - ▪ Disagree and refuse to provide consent for:
  - ▪ Sharing Information from your child's or youth's files with others
  - ▪ Evaluating your child or youth for special needs
  - ▪ Placing your child or youth in special education
  - ▪ Obtaining information from other people/programs about your child or youth
  - ▪ Giving information to another person about your child or youth
  - ▪ Changing the program or your child's or youth's placement
  - ▪ Removing your child or youth from exceptional student services
- ✓ Request a due process hearing on
- ✓ The identification, assessment, or placement of your child or youth
- ✓ The school's refusal to provide a free and appropriate education
- ✓ The right to appeal if the due process does not satisfy your concerns
- ✓ Expect that all information concerning your child will be kept private

THE RIGHTS OF STUDENTS IN SPECIAL EDUCATION

Your child or youth in exceptional education programs has the right to:

- ✓ A free and appropriate public education
- ✓ Related services that will permit them to benefit from special education
- ✓ Access to the same variety of programs and services that other students without special needs enjoy, including non-academic subjects and extracurricular activities like sports and band
- ✓ Placement in a class that has the least restrictions and is most like regular education classes
- ✓ To attend the same school as they would have if they did not need special education services
- ✓ The opportunity to learn even if attending a public school is not possible
- ✓ Participate in the writing if the IEP Plan
- ✓ Placement outside of the school district in another public or private school at public expense if the local schools do not have an appropriate or available program
- ✓ Testing for placement that is free of racial or cultural discrimination
- ✓ An annual review and update of the IEP Plan
- ✓ Remain in their present placement during mediation or a due process hearing
- ✓ School modifications and adaptations that will enhance school success
- ✓ Not be expelled because of behaviors attributed to their disability without due process
- ✓ Privacy and confidentiality of all records

504 Plans

Section 504 is part of a federal civil rights law known as the Rehabilitation Act of 1973. This law prohibits discrimination against persons with a disability. Section 504 prohibits discrimination against students with disabilities and guarantees them a free and appropriate public education (FAPE). For the purposes of this section, discrimination is defined as the failure to provide students with disabilities the same opportunity to benefit from education programs, services, or activities as is provided to their nondisabled peers. Because of this law, schools are not allowed to exclude students with disabilities from facilities, programs, activities, or services that are provided to students without disabilities and schools must make sure that all students receive equal access to educational opportunities. Please note that all students that receive special education services, as defined by the Individuals with Disabilities Education Act (IDEA), are protected under Section 504, but not all students covered under Section 504 are eligible for special education services.

The Rehabilitation Act of 1973 defines a person with a disability as any person who has a physical or mental impairment that substantially limits one or more major life activities, has a record of such impairment, or is regarded as having impairment. Major life activities as defined in the Rehabilitation Act include caring for one's self, performing manual tasks, walking, seeing, hearing, speaking, breathing, learning, and working. Learning does not have to be the major life activity affected in order for an individual to be eligible for protections and services under Section 504.

Just as with the referral process for the IEP, you, a teacher, or other member of the school staff may raise a concern about your child's or youth's unique need for special help. As a result of a "504 referral", you, teachers, and other staff members will meet to discuss all relevant information about your child or youth. Your participation, as a parent, in this meeting is critical and helps to establish an accurate picture of your child or youth's needs. At the meeting, the team will consider whether your child or youth has a disability that substantially limits a major life activity. If the team needs more information, they will request your consent to evaluate your child or youth. If the team determines that your child or youth has a disability, they will then identify what types of support or accommodations are appropriate to meet identified needs.

These accommodations will be described in a document called the "Section 504 Accommodation Plan or simply the "504 Plan".

A 504 Plan describes the accommodations that the school will provide to support your child's or youth's education. While Section 504 does not require a written plan, it does require documentation of evaluations and accommodations. It is very useful to have a written plan to provide clarity and direction to the individuals delivering services or making accommodations for your child or youth. While there is no time limit specified for an accommodation plan, a yearly review is recommended. Section 504 accommodation plans may be updated at any time to reflect changes and recommendations by the team based upon the needs of your child or youth.

What are the major differences between IDEA and Section 504?
Section 504 of the Rehabilitation Act of 1973 provides rights and protections for students with disabilities and includes those students who need accommodations but are not otherwise eligible for special education services under IDEA. Both IDEA and Section 504 guarantee students with disabilities access to a free and appropriate public education. However, there are major differences between Section 504 and IDEA in terms of the criteria used to determine eligibility and the definition of a free and appropriate public education. IDEA identified specific disability categories (e.g. intellectual impairment, deaf or hard-of-hearing, speech or language impairments, visual impairments, emotional/behavioral disabilities, orthopedic impairments, autism spectrum disorder, traumatic brain injury, other health impairments, and specific learning disabilities). For a child or youth to receive exceptional student education services under IDEA, educational performance must be adversely affected by the disability and the child or youth must be in need of special education services (i.e., specialized instruction). Students with a disability who meet specific IDEA requirements are also protected under Section 504. IDEA applies only to individuals from birth through age 21. Section 504 is not limited to specific disability categories and does not require evidence that the disability adversely affects your child's or youth's educational performance. However, the definition states that in order to be eligible for an accommodation plan, they must "have a physical or mental impairment which substantially limits one or more major life activities." Finally, Section 504 covers individuals of all ages.

School Modifications and Adaptations

School adaptations and modifications should be written into your child's or youth's IEP or Section 504 Plan when modifications/adaptations are necessary for your child or youth to succeed in school. It is important to include the student in planning for modifications to learn what they feel would help most. The following are examples of adaptations and modifications that might assist a student with behavioral or mental health needs maximize their success in school.

Textbook and Curriculum Adaptations

Books
- ❑ Alternative books at an easier reading level
- ❑ Audio tapes of textbooks
- ❑ High interest reading material
- ❑ Other: _____

Curriculum
- ❑ Shorter assignments
- ❑ Substitutes for written assignments (like posters, clay models, collections)
- ❑ Change in the percentage of work required for passing grade
- ❑ List of exactly what the student will need to learn(or do) to pass
- ❑ Modify expectations based upon student needs
- ❑ Alternative assignments such as several short reports or oral report rather than one long written report
- ❑ Other: _____

Classroom Modifications
- ❑ Individualized rules for student
- ❑ Classroom structure based on student need (flexibility, size)
- ❑ Keep classroom quiet during intense learning times
- ❑ Reduce visual distractions
- ❑ Seat student by teacher
- ❑ Seat student away from window or doorway
- ❑ Other: _____

Directions

- ❑ Use both oral and written directions
- ❑ Give directions in small steps
- ❑ Have student repeat directions
- ❑ Show a sample of the end product (finished math problem, finished written report)
- ❑ Other: _____

Time/Transitions

- ❑ Alert students several minutes before ending one activity and moving to another
- ❑ Provide additional time to complete task
- ❑ Allow extra time to complete homework, without penalty
- ❑ Other: _____

Other

- ❑ Check progress and provide feedback in first few minutes of assignment
- ❑ Break down long assignments into small steps and monitor progress
- ❑ Reinforce student to record assignments and due dates in notebook
- ❑ Other: _____

Behavior

- ❑ Arrange for a daily check-in time (with the teacher)to organize and review day
- ❑ Pair child or youth with a student with good behavior
- ❑ Eliminate or modify student rules that relate to the disability or medication
- ❑ Amend consequences for rule violations
- ❑ Develop an individualized behavior plan that is consistent with the child's or youth's ability and needs
- ❑ Arrange for student to leave classroom and report to "safe" place when under stress
- ❑ Develop a system or code to use when behavior is becoming inappropriate
- ❑ Ignore behaviors that are not seriously disruptive
- ❑ Other: _____

Grading
- ❑ Provide partial grades on individual progress and effort
- ❑ Use frequent or daily grading rather than waiting for the end of a quarter
- ❑ Weigh daily grade to count more than tests
- ❑ Use pass-fail rather than ABC grades
- ❑ Other: _____

Tests
- ❑ Teach student how to take tests
- ❑ Allow as much time as necessary to take a test
- ❑ Allow tests to be taken in a room with few distractions
- ❑ Have test questions read to student
- ❑ Divide tests into small sections
- ❑ Other: _____

Services and Treatment Information

"We had no idea what we were supposed to do, what was the right treatment or what was not a good idea. We just kept gathering information and tried to learn as much as we could so that when someone said we needed to use a certain medication or treatment we at least had an idea what they were talking about."

There are many types of services available for children and youth with emotional, behavioral, and mental health disorders and their families. The specific types of treatments and services that your child or youth may receive is determined by a combination of factors including professional's perception of your child's or youth's needs; what services and programs are available in your area; and the funding available to pay for appropriate services and programs. Possible treatments and services include, but are not limited to medication, psychotherapy, counseling, in patient or outpatient services and other related supports. This section includes an overview of services, information about medications, and a discussion of how services and treatments may be funded.

Medication

"Everyone had an opinion...give her medication...don't give her medication. Sometimes, even the doctors did not agree. All I know is that it has helped us and she is slowly learning to control her behaviors. Someday, I hope that she will not need the meds."

Many types of medications are used to treat mental health disorders. Medications should be prescribed only after a full evaluation and considering all of the other options available for treating a particular diagnosis. Medications can only be prescribed by a physician. Often the physician who prescribes medications for mental health disorders are a psychiatrist; a physician who has special training in the diagnosis and treatment of mental health disorders. The specific medications that are used depend on the diagnosis and the individual needs of the child or youth being treated.
Medication can help with many problems, but will not "fix" everything. Medications can help with disturbances of mood or attention (such as attention deficit-hyperactivity disorder - ADHD), anxiety, some impulse control problems, and with confused thinking and views. However, medication will not help eliminate a developmental delay or cure a genetic disorder such as Down Syndrome.

How Professionals Know These Are the Right Drugs
Assessing if and what kind of medications will work best for your child or youth is a team effort that includes you and the professionals working with your child or youth. It begins with information sharing and exchange and continues throughout the treatment period. This process should include:

➲ Assessment
    ➲ Inclusion in the Treatment Plan
        ➲ Coordinating Treatment
            ➲ Communication and Record Keeping
                ➲ Special Considerations

Assessment

The purpose of an assessment is to help the treating physician (and other members of the team) to get a better understanding of your child or youth, their particular needs, and the priorities and resources of your family. The assessment process usually starts with the gathering, sharing and review of information that is already available, such as past medical records and the results of past psychological testing. The assessment process should also involve a discussion with your child's or youth's primary care physician, interviews with your child or youth, you, and others who are involved in your child's life, (such as teachers and therapists), as well as a review of all of the important parts of your child's or youth's world. This will assist the team in understanding the role medication could play in helping your child or youth.

Developing a Treatment Plan

Medication given to your child or youth should be a part of the treatment plan. The process of developing a treatment plan builds on the assessment and involves: a) identifying the targeted symptoms: 2) defining a set of time-framed, measurable goals, 3) stating what medications will be used, and 4) describing how the plan will be monitored and evaluated. Monitoring of the plan and medication should include a schedule for documenting and reporting on the targeted symptoms, other behaviors, and adverse outcomes.

By participating in the process of developing the treatment plan, you will:
- Have a better understanding of the desired outcomes from the medication
- Be able to participate more effectively in implementing the overall treatment plan and recognize and report changes in your child's or youth's behavior to the doctor

A medication/medical treatment plan should be written so that it can be easily understood by you and by all other providers with whom it is shared.

Coordinating Treatment

The use of medications should be coordinated with other services and interventions that your child or youth receives. All individuals, professionals, and providers should work together with you to make sure that everyone understands what treatment outcomes are expected and shares important information about your child or youth in a timely fashion. This will help prevent individual team members from unintentionally interfering with overall treatment efforts.

Side Effects of Medication

All medications have the potential for producing side effects, so you should expect that the medications your child or youth is taking for his/her mental health condition will have some side effects. Some side effects are "expected", while other side effects indicate that something may be very wrong. Your child's or youth's treatment plan should include a section about what side effects are "expected' or "acceptable" and what ones are "not acceptable" or may indicate that there is a problem. The treatment plan should also include instructions about what should be done to reduce the negative impact of "unacceptable" side effects on your child or youth and what to do in an emergency.

Medication for the treatment of emotional, mental, and behavioral disorders can cause the following side effects:
- ✓ Feeling overly tired
- ✓ An upset stomach
- ✓ Headaches
- ✓ A dry mouth
- ✓ Constipation
- ✓ Increased or lowered appetite
- ✓ Rashes
- ✓ Tardive dyskinesia (involuntary, repetitive body movements)

It is important for you to discuss and understand what side effects can be expected, how long they might last, and when and how they should be reported to your child's or youth's doctor.

Since too much or too little of a medication can cause problems, doctors can use blood tests to determine how much of some kinds of drug are in your child or youth's system. By measuring the drug in the blood doctors can more accurately adjust the dosage to ensure your child or youth is getting the right amount.

Sometimes these medications can cause more serious side effects. If any of the following are seen, you should contact your child's or youth's doctor immediately.

- Shortness of breath
- Chest discomfort
- Severe agitation
- Fainting
- Disorientation or confusion
- Seizures

If you are uncomfortable with changes in your child or youth that may be due to medication you should discuss it with the doctor as soon as possible.

When the Medication Is Not Working
It is possible that a medication may not work the way it was expected to. Understanding this possibility from the start of treatment will help you from having unrealistic expectations and increase the chances of finding a different, more effective medication for your child or youth. If the team has agreed on the target symptoms and goals, the way to measure progress, and on timeframe in the treatment plan; then the team (the doctor, you , your child or youth, and others) will know when and how to consider other options.

Questions You May Have about Your Child's or Youth's Medication

Below are questions you should ask about every prescribed medication.

- ❑ What is the name of the medication?
- ❑ Is it called by any other name(s)?
- ❑ What is it used for?
- ❑ Is it used for anything other than what it is being used for in my child or youth?
- ❑ Are there other medications you could use instead?
- ❑ Why did you recommend this particular medication?
- ❑ What side effects can be expected?
- ❑ Are there side effects that can affect my child's or youth's school performance?
- ❑ What possible side effects do I need to know about?
- ❑ What side effects should I call about immediately, and what side effects can wait until your office is open?
- ❑ Are there other medications or foods my child or youth should avoid while taking this medication?
- ❑ Are there any activities my child or youth should avoid while taking this medication?
- ❑ How long (days?, weeks?) do you feel my child or youth may need this medication?
- ❑ How will we know if the medication is working?
- ❑ How long (days?, weeks?) might that take before the medication starts to have an effect on my child's or youth's behavior or mood?
- ❑ Will any tests or other blood work have to be done while using this medication?
- ❑ How often and where would these tests be done?
- ❑ When and how should I give the medication?
- ❑ What happens if we miss a dose?
- ❑ Can my child or youth become addicted to this medication?
- ❑ Do you have any written information on this drug?
- ❑ What is the cost of the medication?
- ❑ Is there a less expensive, generic version of this medication?
- ❑ Does the generic work as well as the brand name version of this medication?
- ❑ How will this be written into my child's or youth's treatment plan and shared with others on the care team, including those at school?

Types of Treatment

"I did not know that there would be more than one way to treat his problems. I did not know what the different treatments were or how they worked. I felt helpless in making decisions until I understood what they could each do for him."

Many different types of services are used in the treatment of children and youth with emotional, behavioral, and mental health disorders and their families. The specific treatment services that a child or youth and family will receive may vary by state and also depends on what programs the child or youth and family is eligible for and/or what health insurance plan is providing coverage. However, no matter where you live or what type of insurance you have (or don't have) the plan of care should be responsive to the specific individual needs of your child or youth and the priorities and values of your family. Further, services should be provided in the most normal setting possible, and should maintain your child or youth in an environment that keeps him or her within the context of their own home and community. This is called the "least restrictive environment".

When professionals develop a treatment plan they should explore all available options and tailor the treatment and the setting to the individual needs of your child or youth. Some children and youth and their families will do better with one kind of treatment approach while others may do best with another approach. As the parent, you can play an important role in helping to design the treatment plan and identifying the treatment setting that is best for your child or youth. To do this effectively, you should:

- Learn all you can about the different options within your program or plan
- Talk with members of your child's or youth's professional team about what treatment approaches and settings might work best
- Keep an open mind and learn all you can before making a decision
- Include your child or youth if they are of an age where he or she can participate in the decisions

- Talk with other families who have used some of the options you are considering and see how a particular treatment approach and/or setting worked for them
- Provide feedback on how well the treatment is working so your child's or youth's team can make changes when necessary

 Treatment Settings

Services and treatments are provided is a variety of different settings. Below are some common settings that might be an option for your child or youth.

Home-based services:

Home-based services are those that are delivered in your home. Often in-home therapy focuses on teaching your family how to deal with certain behaviors and problems. In-home services are considered to be an essential element of a comprehensive approach to addressing the needs of children and youth with emotional, behavioral, or mental health disorders.

School based services

Services for your child or youth and your family may be provided at your child's or youth's school. These services may be part of a school program, or may be a "related service" like a workshop or support group that uses the school setting as a convenient delivery site. Schools are required by law to provide students with emotional, behavioral, or mental health disorders with appropriate special education services if the mental health problem is interfering with the student's learning. These educational efforts are regulated by laws and must be based upon an individualized education plan (IEP) that is jointly developed by the school and you. Special education services that are included in the IEP must be provided at no cost to you. See the section on Education for more information.

Community based services

Some services and treatment programs are located in your community. These services allow your child or youth to remain in the community and at home while receiving treatment. This type of service includes day treatment programs and outpatient counseling/psychotherapy.

Residential treatment services

Residential services provide around the clock treatment, medication supervision, and careful monitoring of behaviors to children and youth who require intensive supervision and a place to live other than at home. There are several forms of residential services, from therapeutic foster care to hospitalization.

 Treatment Methods

The goal of treatment is to reduce the symptoms associated with a disorder, improve personal and social functioning, develop and strengthen coping skills, and promote behaviors that will make a child's or youth's life better. Treatment methods can be classified as being one of three types: psychotropic therapy, psychotherapy, and behavioral therapy. Each type of treatment can be used alone or in various combinations. All methods may not be available through every program or insurance plan. There may also be treatments that are not available in your area due to a lack of qualified professionals.

Psychotropic Therapies (Medication)

Psychotropic treatment uses medications to benefit children and youth with emotional, behavioral, and mental disorders and is often combined with other therapy. The medication that a psychiatrist or other physician prescribes depends on the nature of your child's or youth's disorder. (See the previous section on medication)

Psychotherapy

This form of therapy involves face-to-face discussions during which a therapist helps children and youth talk about and resolve issues, behaviors, and emotional problems. Short-term psychotherapy (lasting several weeks or months) may be used when a problem seems to result from a stressful life event such as a death in the family, divorce, or physical illness. In short-term therapy, the goal is to help the child or youth resolve the problem as quickly as possible. Often this takes only a few visits. Long-term psychotherapy (lasting from several months to several years), is used to address chronic, underlying and more serious problems.

Types of psychotherapy include (but are not limited to):

- **Psychodynamic psychotherapy** examines important relationships and experiences from early childhood to the present to analyze and change unsettling or destructive behaviors and to resolve emotional problems.
- **Interpersonal therapy** focuses on the child's or youth's current life and relationships within the family, social, and school or work environments.
- **Family therapy** involves discussions and problem-solving sessions with every member of a family - as a group or with individual family members.
- **Group therapy** involves a small group of people with similar problems who, with the guidance of a therapist, discuss individual issues and help each other with problems.
- **Play therapy** is used for establishing communication and resolving problems with young children.
- **Cognitive therapy** corrects distorted thinking patterns that can lead to troublesome feelings and behaviors. Cognitive therapy is often combined effectively with behavioral therapy.

Behavioral Therapy

Behavioral therapy helps children and youth to learn acceptable behaviors that replace those that are unacceptable. This approach can involve family members giving praise and attention to desirable changes in behavior.

Counseling

A clinical mental health counselor provides professional counseling services that may involve psychotherapy to help children, youth and families.

Adjunctive Treatments

"Adjunctive," treatments include occupational, recreational, art and other creative therapies, as well as those that focus on special education. These are typically used in combination with other therapies, but are sometimes used alone.

Types of Mental Health Professionals

Psychiatrists are medical doctors who specialize in mental disorders, are licensed to practice medicine, and have completed a year of internship and three years of specialty training in psychiatry. A board-certified psychiatrist has, in addition, practiced the profession for at least two years and passed the written and oral examinations of the American Board of Psychiatry and Neurology. Psychiatrists can evaluate and diagnose all types of mental disorders, carry out biomedical treatments and psychotherapy, and work with psychological problems associated with medical disorders. "Child psychiatrists" specialize in working with children. Only medical doctors, including psychiatrists, can prescribe medications.

Psychologists may conduct psychotherapy, work with individuals, groups, or families to resolve problems, and are generally called clinical psychologists. The practice of psychology may include psychological testing, evaluation, counseling, psychoanalysis, psychotherapy, hypnosis, biofeedback, and behavioral analysis and therapy. Psychologists work in many settings; for example, in mental health centers, hospitals and clinics, schools, and private practice. A licensed clinical psychologist has met the state's requirements for licensure, which typically includes having a doctoral degree (Ph.D.) in psychology.

Clinical social workers have either a master's degree or a doctoral degree in social work, have completed a field supervision program, and are licensed or certified. In addition to individual, family, and group counseling and psychotherapy, they are trained in client advocacy. This includes information, referral, direct intervention with governmental and civic agencies, and expansion of community resources.

Mental health counselors provide professional counseling services that involve psychotherapy, human development, learning theory, and group dynamics to help individuals, couples, and families. The promotion and enhancement of healthy, satisfying lifestyles are the goals of mental health counselors, whether the services are provided in a mental health center, business, private practice, or other community agency. Clinical mental health counselors have earned at least a master's degree, had supervised experience, and passed a national examination before they can be certified by the National Board for Certified Counselors, Inc.

Certified Behavior Analysts use behavior analysis to assist children and youth in learning new behaviors and changing existing behaviors that often produce bad outcomes.

Questions You May Have about Your Child's or Youth's Treatment

When it is suggested that your child or youth receive treatment for an emotional, behavioral, or mental health disorder, you should ask questions to help you understand the treatment and the impact it may have on your family. Below are some questions you should ask BEFORE treatment is started.

- ❑ What type of treatment is this?
- ❑ Why does my child or youth need it?
- ❑ What types of changes in my child or youth and family can I expect as a result of this treatment?
- ❑ Where will my child or youth receive this treatment?
- ❑ How often and for how long will the treatment be necessary?
- ❑ Can I get a second opinion?
- ❑ How much will this treatment cost?
- ❑ Will my health insurance plan pay for the treatment?
- ❑ What other treatment options are available?
- ❑ Is this the least restrictive option for my child or youth?
- ❑ What will our role be in the treatment and developing the treatment plan?
- ❑ How often can we visit, phone, or contact our child or youth? (for inpatient services)
- ❑ What would be the next step after this treatment is completed?
- ❑ What are the credentials, training, experience, and reputation of those providing services?
- ❑ Will you or a member of your staff assist me in checking to see if the program or facility has violated any licensing laws?
- ❑ Can I decide to stop the treatment at any time I feel that it is necessary?
- ❑ Can you put me in touch with another family that has used this particular treatment, program or facility?

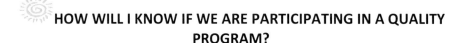

HOW WILL I KNOW IF WE ARE PARTICIPATING IN A QUALITY PROGRAM?

There are many programs and service providers to assist families of children and youth with emotional, behavioral, or mental health disorders. To be sure that the services that your child or youth and family are receiving are good enough complete the following survey.   You should be able to answer "yes" to nearly all of these questions. The fewer times you need to answer "no", the better the service. If the program or services you use receive a "no" answer, make a special effort to discuss the things you feel are important in a quality program with your providers and identify ways they can assist you in meeting your child or youth's needs.

	YES	NO
Decisions are made about my child or youth with my input.		
My family schedule is considered when making appointments, meetings.		
All members of my family are invited to meetings, appointments, etc.		
The culture and beliefs of my family are respected by all staff.		
I am not blamed for the problems my child or youth has.		
The staff uses words I can understand.		
I am asked if I have questions or concerns.		
The results of tests and evaluations are shared and explained to me.		
I am comfortable telling the staff "no" when I disagree with them.		
I am asked how well I like the services we are getting.		
I receive information about services in a language I can understand.		
I received information on how to resolve conflicts or disagreements with the program.		
I am told how long I could expect to be involved with the service.		
I know who to call and can contact someone when I have questions.		
I get regular updates on how well my child or youth is doing.		
I have a copy of a care/treatment plan.		
Specific goals were set up for my family and child or youth and support was provided to help us achieve these goals.		
The staff communicates with other programs/services my family receives.		
I feel like this service is making a positive impact in my child's or youth's life.		
I would recommend this service to other families.		
TOTAL		

HOW WILL I KNOW IF OUR PROGRAM IS CULTURALLY RESPONSIBLE?

It is important that the programs that serve your family recognize and respect your culture, family values, and traditions. Below are some questions that you can ask yourself about the cultural and linguistic competence of the services. You should be able to answer "yes" to nearly all of these questions. The fewer times you need to answer "no" the more sensitive the service is to your culture and beliefs. If the program or services you use receive a "no" answer, make an effort to discuss with them the things you feel are important to you and your family. If you are uncomfortable doing this, ask another member of your culture to do it for you.

	YES	NO
All information is shared in a language we can understand		
Our cultural holidays, traditions, and beliefs are considered when making appointments and meetings.		
Other persons important to our family are included in meetings, appointments, etc.		
Our culture and beliefs are never joked about by staff.		
Our culture is not blamed for the problems of our child or youth.		
The staff offers translations we can understand.		
We are asked how the services we receive can impact our culture and beliefs.		
We are encouraged to include our beliefs and culture into the service plan.		
The staff respects us when we disagree with them based upon our culture/beliefs.		
We are asked if there are any conflicts between our beliefs and planned services.		
The program has no policies that insult our culture or beliefs.		
The staff shows an interest in learning about our family's culture.		
Staff represents the cultures and populations served by the program.		
We are comfortable telling the staff about our beliefs.		
Our beliefs are considered, even when we are not present.		
We would recommend this service to other families of our culture.		
TOTAL		

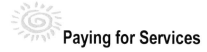 **Paying for Services**

One of the most difficult challenges facing families of children and youth with emotional or mental health disorders is paying for or finding funding to pay for the service their child or youth needs. Expenses often exceed the amount paid by their health insurance plan, especially if frequent hospitalizations are necessary.   Other funding sources may be available, but these are often overwhelmed with requests for help. Families must learn how to locate and understand all sources of funding, so that they will be able to pay for the services and supports that their child needs. Sources of payment for services include:

Insurance
You may have health insurance through your employer or you may purchase a plan privately. Insurance companies determine what services they pay for, how much they pay for specific services, how services are delivered, and the treatment settings in which they will pay for selected services. Insurance companies have standards and require that all services be of quality, medically necessary, and delivered in the most cost-effective manner.

Title XIX/Medicaid
Medicaid is a partnership between the federal government and the states. Under this program, the federal government reimburses each state for a portion of its cost for providing medical care to children and youth from low income families. States agree to provide a specified package of services in return for the money they get from the federal government. Each state has the right to determine if some types of services will (or will not) be offered through their Medicaid program. All Medicaid service must be determined to medically necessary and approved by a physician who participates in the state Medicaid program.

Children's Health Insurance Program (S/CHIP)
The SCHIP program is administered by the US Department of Health and Human Services and provides funds to States to have health insurance available to otherwise uninsured families with children. The program is supposed to cover uninsured children and youth in families with incomes that are too high to qualify for Medicaid and that do not have other

insurance resources. Like Medicaid, SCHIP is a partnership between federal and state governments. The programs are run by the individual states according to requirements set by the federal Centers for Medicare and Medicaid Services (CMS). States may design their SCHIP programs within certain limits, so each state's SCHIP may look a little different.

Others-Some families have access to other resources to pay for their child's or youth's services and treatments. Some of these are based upon community based programs, state programs, military or employee benefits, or others.

Notes

Resources

ED.gov

1-800-USA-LEARN (1-800-872-5327)
http://www2.ed.gov/about/offices/list/osers/osep/index.html?src=mr
Office of Special Education and Rehabilitative Services (OSERS) and Office of Special Education Programs (OSEP)
OPEP is dedicated to improving results for infants, toddlers, children and youth with disabilities ages birth through 21 by providing leadership and financial support to assist states and local districts.

Family Voices

(505) 872-4774
Toll Free: (888) 835-5669
www.familyvoices.org
Family Voices aims to achieve family-centered care for all children and youth with special health care needs and/or disabilities, including those with mental, emotional, and behavioral disorders. Through a national network, Family Voices provides families with tools to make informed decisions, advocate for improved public and private policies, build partnerships among professionals and families, and serve as a trusted resource on health care.

National Federation of Families for Children's Mental Health-FFCMH

240-403-1901
www.ffcmh.org
The National Federation, a national family-run organization, provides advocacy at the national level for the rights of children and youth with emotional, behavioral and mental health challenges and their families, leadership and technical assistance to a nation-wide network of family run organizations, and collaborates with family run and other child serving organizations to transform mental health care in America

Mental Health America-MHA

(703) 684-7722

www.nmha.org

Mental Health America – MHA is the nation's largest and oldest community-based network dedicated to helping all Americans live mentally healthier lives. With our more than 300 affiliates across the country, MHA touches the lives of millions—**Advocating** for changes in policy; **Educating** the public & providing critical information; & delivering urgently needed **Programs and Services**.

National Alliance for the Mentally Ill-NAMI

(703) 524-7600

www.nami.org

The National Alliance for the Mentally Ill - NAMI is a national, grassroots mental health advocacy organization. The NAMI organization operates at the local, state and national levels. Each level of the organization provides support, education, information and referral and advocacy to support Americans who live with serious mental illness today and their families.

TA Partnership for Child and Family Mental Health

(202) 403-6827

www.tapartnership@air.org

The Technical Assistance Partnership for Child and Family Mental Health (TA Partnership) provides technical assistance to system of care communities that are currently funded through the Comprehensive Community Mental Health Services for Children and their Families Program.

Substance Abuse and Mental Health Services Administration-SAMHSA

1-877-SAMHSA-7 (1-877-726-4727)

http://www.samhsa.gov/families/index.aspx

SAMHSA's goal is to improve outcomes for children and youth with and/or at risk for mental, substance use and/or co-occurring disorders, and their families by increasing access to a continuum of comprehensive, integrated, culturally and linguistically competent services and supports that include prevention, early intervention, treatment, and recovery.

Glossary

Access	The ability to get services for people who need them in a way that encourages their use
Assessment	A professional review of a child and family's strengths and needs; includes a review of child's mental and physical status, educational performance, intelligence, family situation, and review of community resources
Accountability	A procedure based on outcomes through which the process of care, the service providers, and/or network is evaluated
Behavioral Health Care	Care provided for the treatment of mental and/or substance abuse disorders
Caregiver	A person who provides basic care to a child, usually the parents, but can be a relative or service provider
Case Management	A process by which the services provided to a specific individual/family are coordinated and managed to achieve the best outcome in the most cost-effective manner
Child Protective Services	Agency/program designed to protect children when there are reports of abuse, neglect, or abandonment, or where there is no family to care for the child; goals include helping the family find resources to address needs to enable the child to remain at home with family
Community Based	Care that responds to the needs identified by the community and draws from that community to address those needs with services provided as near to the home as possible
Comprehensive Care	A system of care that covers primary (including prevention), secondary, and tertiary care and addresses physical health, mental health, nutrition, and oral health; integrates health and health related services with education, social services, and family support systems
Continuity of Care	Comprehensive care that is provided during all transitions, such as hospital to home, home to hospital, etc.; planning ensures linkages with education, health, and community resources
Consumer	A person who receives and/or purchases services while also advocating for service quality and appropriateness
Consumer Satisfaction	The evaluation concerning how well a consumer, family, child, or youth liked the services they received and/or the manner in which they were provided
Continuum of Care	An array of services that meets the needs of a specific group or population in an appropriate and cost-effective manner
Coordination of	A system that assures services are delivered in an organized

Care	fashion and assure the timeliness, appropriateness, continuity, and completeness of care
Co-payment	Specified amount that an insured individual must pay when receiving a covered service
Culturally Competent	The system of care that honors and respects culturally related beliefs, values, interpersonal styles, attitudes, and behaviors of families; respect for those values is incorporated at all levels of policy, administration, and practice
Day Treatment	Treatment that lasts less than four hours per day and may include special education, counseling, vocational training, skill building, or specific therapies
DSM	Diagnostic and Statistical Manual of Mental Disorders, an official manual used by mental health professionals to understand and diagnose mental health disorders
Early Intervention	Providing services to prevent further deterioration, delay
Emergency/Crisis Services	A group of services available 24 hours a day, 7 days a week to help during a mental health emergency
Fee-for-service	A payment system that pays providers for each unit of service
Gate Keeping	The use of primary care clinicians, case managers or some other mechanism as the initial contact for care to ensure that patients use care in an appropriate and cost-effective care way
Home Based Services	Help or services provided in a child's or youth's home
Individualized Services	Services that are based on the individual needs of the child, youth, or family; rather than on what a program has to offer or on a diagnosis
Lead Agency	An organization that has clinical and fiscal authority to provide and/or subcontract for services that address document patient goals or outcome objectives
Local Mental Health	Local organization (usually with statutory authority) that maintains central administrative, clinical and fiscal authority for an organized system of behavioral health care
Long-term Outcome	The result of care over time, as opposed to more immediate (short term)effects
Managed Care Organization (MCO)	An organization that provides a managed health care plan
Mental Health	Refers to how a person thinks, feels, and acts when faced with life's situations
Mental Health Disorder	Problems that effect one's thoughts, body, feelings, and behavior

Medicaid	A federal program that is administered by each participating state and shares in program costs to provide medical benefits to specific groups of low income and/or categorically eligible persons
Medical Necessity	A specific health care service that is medically appropriate, necessary to meet the person's health needs, consistent with the person's diagnosis, and consistent with established standards of care
Outcomes	The results of a specific health care service
Participating Provider	A provider who has contracted with a health plan to provide specific services
Payer /Payor	The public or private organization that is responsible for the payment of health care expenses
Plan of Care	A treatment plan for a child, youth, or family that specifically outlines goals and the services necessary to reach them
Preferred Provider Organization (PPO)	An organization which contracts with specified physicians and other professionals to provide health care services to individuals enrolled in a their health plan and uses incentives to encourage enrollees to use the services of contracted providers
Premium	The amount of money paid to a health plan to provide coverage over a specified time period
Primary Care Physician	A physician or clinician whose practice focuses upon internal medicine, family/general practice, pediatrics and obstetrics/gynecology
Prior-Authorization	A procedure used to screen the value of services by reviewing requests for services prior to the service being provided
Provider	An organization or individual that provides and is reimbursed for a health care service
Quality Assurance	Efforts to review and improve the quality of services provided
Residential Treatment	Facilities that provide treatment 24 hours per day and can usually serve more than 12 individuals at a time, may also be known as therapeutic group homes
Respite Care	Service that provides a break for parents who have a child or youth with special needs; service can be provided in the child's home or in a specialized care setting
Service Provider	One who provides services; can be a school, doctor, therapist, etc.
SSA	Social Security Administration that oversees SSI and SSDI (see below)
SSI	Supplemental Security Income, paid to eligible recipients to offset income loss due to a disability

SSDI	Social Security Disability Income, set dollar amount paid to eligible persons and their dependents when they have lost their jobs due to a disability
Stakeholders	Groups of persons with a special interest in the design and operations of a service or product; stakeholders include consumers, family members of consumers, service providers, legislators
State Mental Health Authority or Agency	State government agency charged with administering and funding a state's public mental health services
Title V (5)	Section of Social Security Act that focuses on Maternal and Child Health. Supports state programs and other initiatives that focuses on health issues of women and children
Title XVIII (18)	Section of Social Security Act that focuses on Medicare
Title XIX (19)	Section of the Social Security Act that focuses on Medicaid
Transitional Services	Services that assist the child and family make a move from one setting or program to another, especially from pediatric (child and youth) to adult services
Utilization	The level of use of a service over time
Wrap-around	Benefits organized around an individual enrollee's needs and has a no-eject, no-reject policy with services continuing as long as beneficial and necessary with a special focus on outcomes rather than cost

The Axis Group I began as a consulting firm that quickly evolved into a corporation with multiple partners, assets, resources, tools, and services. The Axis Group I, LLC is determined to improve the capacity of consumers, families, communities, and the programs that serve them through training, information, and resources; promoting systems that are responsive to the people they serve and populations with the capacity to participate as system transformation change agents.

The Axis Group I, LLC grew out of recognition that if families and their children and youth, consumers, and the programs and organizations that serve them are going to meet their goals, then new resources, approaches, and tools would be needed. Key to the development of these resources and tools is a gathering and sharing of the experience and expertise of those that have navigated the system. It is this experience, this expertise, and this voice that drives the work of the Axis Group I.

For more resources, tools, information, and services contact us at:

Axis Group I, LLC

www.axisgroup1.net
cjwellls@axisgroup1.net

All Rights Reserved

Watch for our upcoming book for professionals...

✳✳✳

More Straight Talk:

Families Speak to Professionals about Child and Youth Mental Health